CAMPAIGN • 212

THE SIX DAY WAR 1967: SINAI

SIMON DUNSTAN   ILLUSTRATED BY PETER DENNIS

Series editors Marcus Cowper and Nikolai Bogdanovic

First published in Great Britain in 2009 by Osprey Publishing,
Midland House, West Way, Botley, Oxford OX2 0PH, UK
443 Park Avenue South, New York, NY 10016, USA
E-mail: info@ospreypublishing.com

A CIP catalogue record for this book is available from the British Library

ISBN: 978 1 84603 363 6
E-book ISBN: 978 1 84908 110 8

Editorial by Ilios Publishing Ltd, Oxford, UK (www.iliospublishing.com)
Page layout by: The Black Spot
Index by Alan Thatcher
Typeset in Sabon and Myriad Pro
Maps by Bounford.com
3D bird's-eye views by The Black Spot
Battlescene illustrations by Peter Dennis
Originated by PDQ Media
Printed in China through Worldprint Ltd

09 10 11 12 13   10 9 8 7 6 5 4 3 2 1

ACKNOWLEDGEMENTS

The author wishes to express his gratitude to Lieutenant-Colonel (Retd.) George Forty OBE for his kind assistance in the preparation of this book. Equally important has been the contribution of Colonel David Eshel, a veteran of the elite 7th Armored Brigade and a distinguished historian of the IDF for many years. During the 1970s and 1980s, he built up a remarkable archive covering every campaign of the IDF. Much of this was published in book form under the imprint Born in Battle. Virtually all the personal accounts related in this volume come from the archives of Born in Battle. These now reside in the museum at the IDF Armored Corps Memorial Site at Latrun – Yad La'Shiryon. My thanks also go to Devori Borger, the museum curator at Latrun, for her unstinting efforts in finding documents and information over many months. All the photographs are courtesy of the Israel Government Press Office. The reader is referred to the bibliography for the secondary sources. Of these the two books by Jeremy Bowen *Six Days* and Michael B. Oren *Six Days of War* are highly recommended to the serious students of military history to place the Six Day War within its political and historical context.

ARTIST'S NOTE

THE WOODLAND TRUST

Osprey Publishing are supporting the Woodland Trust, the UK's leading woodland conservation charity, by funding the dedication of trees.

Key to military symbols

Key to unit identification

CONTENTS

The Middle East in 1967

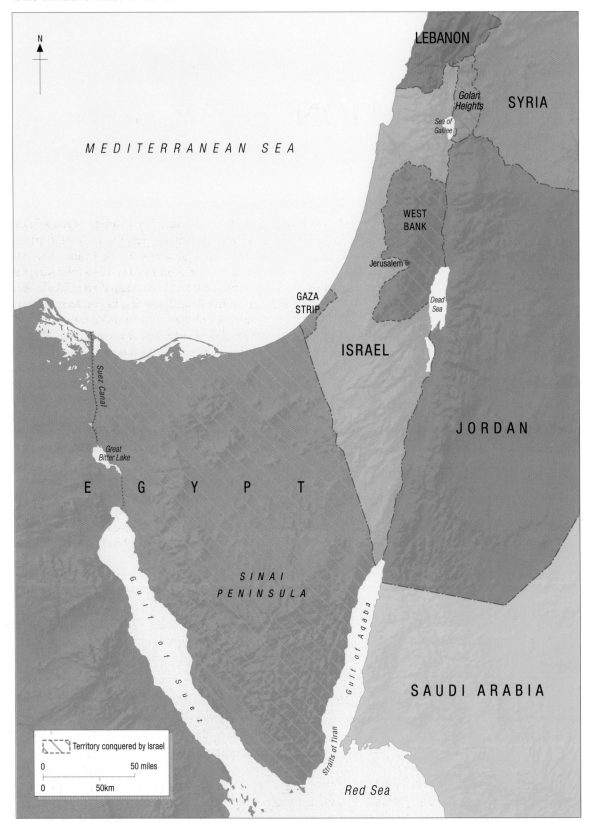

N

LEBANON

SYRIA

Golan
Heights

Sea of
Galilee

MEDITERRANEAN SEA

WEST
BANK

Jerusalem

GAZA
STRIP

Dead
Sea

ISRAEL

JORDAN

Suez Canal

Great
Bitter Lake

E G Y P T

SINAI
PENINSULA

Gulf of Suez

Gulf of Aqaba

SAUDI ARABIA

Straits of Tiran

Red Sea

Territory conquered by Israel

0   50 miles

0   50km

INTRODUCTION

The Third Arab-Israeli War of June 1967 was caused by a variety of geopolitical factors. Taken in isolation, none was sufficiently serious to justify armed conflict between countries that were all signatories to the United Nations Charter of 1945. The state of Israel was created on 14 May 1948 following the end of the British Mandate for Palestine that had been created after World War I. In the following days, the armies of five Arab countries, Egypt, Iraq, Jordan, Lebanon and Syria, invaded the territory of the newly founded nation. To the Israelis the First Arab-Israeli War of 1948–49 was known as the War of Independence. In a desperate war for survival, the 15-month conflict claimed the lives of over 6,000 Israelis or almost one per cent of the total population. Following UN Resolution 181, the remainder of the Palestine Mandate was divided between the Jews and the Arabs with Israel receiving just 13 per cent of the original area of the British Mandate with 60 per cent of that land comprising the arid Negev Desert. Following the conflict, Egypt occupied the Gaza Strip and Transjordan annexed a sizeable area to the west of the Jordan River that became known as the West Bank within the Hashemite Kingdom of Jordan. Fundamental to three of the world's great religions, Jerusalem remained a divided city. Meanwhile, Israel unilaterally occupied the port of Eilat on the Gulf of Aqaba to give her access to the Red Sea thus splitting the two Arab countries of Egypt and Jordan. All these areas were to become points of serious friction in the years to come. No Arab nation recognized the state of Israel or even its right to exist.

The camouflage nets are unveiled from the M48A2C Pattons of the 79th Tank Battalion of 7th Armored Brigade in their forming-up positions in the Negev Desert just prior to the Six Day War.

CHRONOLOGY

1952

23 July Revolution in Egypt conducted by the armed forces orchestrated by the Free Officers Movement including Colonel Gamal Abd el Nasser and Major Abd el Hakim Amer.

1954

7 April Colonel Nasser assumes power from General Muhammad Naguib and becomes President of Egypt in October.

1956

26 July President Nasser nationalizes Suez Canal. He also orders the blocking of the Straits of Tiran to Israeli shipping.

29 October The Second Arab-Israeli War breaks out with the Israel Defense Forces (IDF) conquering the Sinai Peninsula within 100 hours.

31 October The Anglo-French military expedition to reoccupy the Suez Canal begins but is forced to withdraw following international pressure by the US and USSR. By March 1957, Israel withdraws after the United Nations Emergency Force (UNEF) deploys to Sinai and Gaza. The US guarantees the right of passage for Israeli shipping through the Straits of Tiran. The Suez Canal reopens on 23 March 1957.

1957

23 February US memorandum guarantees freedom of passage through the Suez Canal for international shipping. On 23 February a revised memorandum states that US would allow use of force to keep the Straits of Tiran open. However, US later claims that these memoranda were 'lost'.

1959

Summer Al-Fatah founded in Kuwait by Yasser Arafat and others to conduct terrorist operations inside Israel.

1964

28 May The Palestine Liberation Organization (PLO) founded following First Arab Summit in Cairo of 13–17 January 1964. The PLO is created as a rival to Fatah to conduct terrorist acts against Israel as Fatah rejects the pan-Arabism of Nasser.

5 June Israel begins pumping water from the Sea of Galilee for the Israel National Water Carrier to divert water to the arid Negev Desert.

13 September Second Arab Summit at Alexandria decides on diversion of the headwaters of the Jordan River to deprive Israel of water as well as strengthening regional Arab armies. Arabs reaffirm their aim of destroying Israel.

1965

2 January Fatah conducts first sabotage raid in Israel against the Israel National Water Carrier. Between January 1965 and June 1967, Fatah carries out approximately 122 raids of which almost 80 per cent were thwarted by the Israeli security forces.

1966

9 November Egypt and Syria sign mutual defence treaty with Egyptian commitment to attack Israel if Israel attacks Syria.

10 November Three IDF soldiers killed in mine incident on Jordanian border.

13 November The IDF retaliate with a major raid on Jordanian village of Samu in the West Bank. It results in growing support for the PLO. King Hussein of Jordan demands military action by Egypt.

14 December Field Marshal Abd el Hakim Amer recommends to Nasser the closing of the Straits of Tiran to Israeli shipping and dismissing the UNEF force from Gaza.

1967

January–March Over 270 border incidents of terrorist attacks and artillery barrages with most originating from Syria cause growing concern in Israel.

7 April Israel retaliates to Syrian shelling of Demilitarized Zone (DMZ) and Israeli villages with raid by the Israeli Air Force (IAF). An aerial battle develops with the Israelis destroying six Syrian MiG-21s.

13 May Soviets pass false intelligence to Anwar Sadat in Moscow that Israel is massing 11 brigades on border for attack on Syria, supposedly to take place on 17 May.

14 May In response, the Egyptian Army deploys two divisions to the Sinai Peninsula.

15 May	Israel celebrates Independence Day sombrely with minimal military presence.
18 May	President Nasser orders the UNEF to leave Gaza. Secretary-General U Thant removes the complete UNEF from the Sinai and Gaza.
20 May	IDF begin mobilization.
23 May	President Nasser closes the Straits of Tiran to Israeli shipping. Egypt reinforces its troop deployment to the Sinai.
30 May	Jordan signs mutual defence pact with Egypt. The IDF complete mobilization.
2 June	General Moshe Dayan joins Israeli cabinet as Minister of Defense.
5 June: Day 1	0745hrs: IAF undertakes pre-emptive strike against Egyptian air bases with Operation *Moked*.
	0800hrs: IDF begin ground operations in Sinai.
	0945hrs: Jordan begins bombardment of Israeli towns and military targets.
	1245hrs: Israel responds with Operation *Moked* attacking Jordanian, Iraqi and Syrian airbases.
	1500hrs: IDF begin ground operations in West Bank with Operation *Whip*.
6 June: Day 2	Southern Command achieves significant successes in Sinai.
	0530hrs: IDF enter Jenin in West Bank.
	0545hrs: Syrian Army bombards Israeli border communities and begins minor ground operation that fails.
	0600hrs: major tank battle in Dothan Valley in West Bank.
	1300hrs: Jenin surrenders.
	1700hrs: battle of Dothan Valley ends.
	2000hrs: Egyptian Army begins general retreat in Sinai.
	2400hrs: Jordanian Army begins general retreat from West Bank across Jordan River.
7 June: Day 3	Syrian bombardment of Israeli villages continues along northern border.
	1000hrs: IDF conquer Old Jerusalem and troops arrive at Western Wall.

1200hrs: Israeli Navy occupies Sharm el Sheikh.

1930hrs: IDF conquer Jericho.

2000hrs: Gidi and Mitla passes sealed by IDF trapping remnants of Egyptian Army in Sinai.

2200hrs: Jordan accepts UN-sponsored ceasefire.

8 June: Day 4 Syrian artillery bombardment continues along northern border.

0630hrs: IDF conquer Hebron.

0800hrs: IDF troops of Central and Southern commands link up at Dahirieh, west of Hebron.

1300hrs: IAF destroys bridges over Jordan River.

1400hrs: IAF and Israeli Navy mount sustained attack against American intelligence-gathering ship USS *Liberty* off coast of Sinai.

1530hrs: Egypt accepts UN-sponsored ceasefire.

9 June: Day 5 0100hrs: IDF troops reach Suez Canal.

1130hrs: IDF undertakes Operation *Hammer* against Syria. 8th Armored Brigade and 1st Golani Infantry Brigade achieve significant successes against Syrian Army.

10 June: Day 6 Syrian Army collapses under IDF offensive.

1830hrs: ceasefire is declared to end hostilities.

12 June IDF occupies the strategic position of Mount Hermon in final act of the war.

19 June Israeli cabinet decides to offer Arabs the return of the conquered territories in exchange for a lasting peace treaty.

1 July Hostilities resume along Suez Canal.

23 August General Moshe Dayan is allowed to name the recent conflict. He calls it 'The Six Day War' with its distinct Biblical connotations.

1 September At a summit in Khartoum, the Arabs declare resolution of 'The three Nos' signifying: No peace with Israel; No recognition of Israel; No negotiations with Israel.

22 November UN Security Council promulgates Resolution 242 demanding Israeli withdrawal from the occupied territories in exchange for peace.

OPPOSING PLANS

EGYPT – A STRATEGY OF RHETORIC

After the Revolutionary Command Council assumed power in Egypt in July 1952, Colonel Gamal Abd el Nasser subsequently emerged as Prime Minister and then President. Initially there was little friction with Israel beyond an unstated policy of 'no war, no peace'. By 1954 this had changed to a more aggressive stance with demands for the return of the port of Eilat and then for the whole of the Negev Desert. These were totally unacceptable to the Israelis. Tension rose dramatically following a massive procurement of Soviet arms by Egypt. The outcome was the Second Arab-Israeli War of 1956 following the nationalization of the Suez Canal with the Israel Defense Forces (IDF) triumphant in the Sinai Peninsula. However, the abortive Anglo-French invasion of the Suez Canal Zone allowed Nasser to claim a resounding victory over the two imperialist powers that had dominated the Middle East since the Great War. Colonel Nasser's stock increased significantly across the Arab world despite the dire performance of the Egyptian armed forces in the recent conflict. His prestige was enhanced further when Israel withdrew from the Sinai Peninsula and Gaza Strip after intensive pressure from the United States and the Soviet Union. Nasser now assumed the mantle as the leader of a pan-Arab movement. His aim was to impose Arab unity across the region under his control. His methodology was to foment internal unrest in various Arab countries, notably Jordan and Lebanon. With the rise to power of the Ba'ath Party in Syria in February 1958,

Typical of the vitriolic propaganda campaign waged against Israel prior to the Six Day War was this cartoon published in the Lebanese newspaper *al-Hayat* showing a Semitic figure representing Israel being pierced and killed by tanks of Egypt, Syria, Jordan and Lebanon.

Nasser persuaded Syria to unite with Egypt as the 'United Arab Republic', acting as two pincers to the north and south of Israel.

In September 1960, Nasser's agents orchestrated the assassination of the Jordanian Prime Minister Hazza al-Majali, a close friend of King Hussein of Jordan. The king himself became the target of repeated assassination attempts masterminded by Colonel Fuad Serag el Din, the Syrian chief of intelligence. In September 1961, Nasser's pan-Arab dream suffered a serious blow when another *coup d'état* in Syria resulted in the collapse of the United Arab Republic. In the following year, Nasser committed Egyptian troops to the Yemen Civil War as a counter to the royalist forces supported by Saudi Arabia. When his forces became bogged down, he resorted to the use of poison gas against his Arab brothers: a fact duly noted by Israeli military intelligence. In 1963, Nasser joined with President Abdul Salam Arif of Iraq in proclaiming 'The aim of the Arabs is the destruction of Israel.' In the following year, the Palestine Liberation Organization (PLO) was formed as a terrorist group to confront the state of Israel under covert Egyptian direction. Meanwhile the diversion of the headwaters of the Jordan River continued apace to deny Israel much of its fresh water. Israel reiterated its position that both the diversion of the Jordan waters and the closing of the Straits of Tiran were tantamount to acts of war or *casus belli*. There ensued prolonged tank and artillery engagements to destroy the engineer plant equipment used to divert the waters, culminating in heavy attacks by the Israeli Air Force (IAF) on 13 November 1964 that initiated the Water War of 1965/66. All the while the rhetoric continued with President Nasser declaiming on 8 March 1965 'We shall not enter Palestine with its soil covered in sand, we shall enter it with its soil saturated in blood.' Throughout 1966, the terrorist attacks of al-Fatah and the PLO inflicted a steady stream of Israeli casualties leading to retaliation raids by the IDF. An attack codenamed Operation *Shredder* on the village of Samu in the Hebron Hills on 13 November 1966 caused severe unrest in Jordan and such heavy criticism of King Hussein that his regime seemed to be on the edge of collapse. Emboldened by the signing of a mutual defence pact between Egypt and Syria on 9 November 1966, the Syrian Army shelling of the farms and kibbutzim below the Golan Heights increased significantly. Inevitably it incurred Israeli wrath culminating in the IAF attacking Syrian artillery emplacements on 7 April 1967. There followed an aerial battle in which six Syrian MiG-21 fighters were shot down, including two over the outskirts of the capital Damascus. Both Jordan and Syria demanded decisive action from Egypt following these incursions into their sovereign territory. As the self-appointed leader of pan-Arabism and fearful of losing face, Nasser was obliged to act yet with almost a quarter of his regular army deployed in Yemen he was hardly in a position to confront Israel militarily. Accordingly, he adopted a policy of brinkmanship whereby he could be seen to be challenging Israel without resorting to armed conflict. It was a strategy fraught with hazard.

The catalyst for disaster

By May 1967, the rhetoric on all sides was becoming more strident. Arab unity remained as elusive as ever when Nasser described King Hussein as 'an agent and slave of the imperialists'. Egypt's relations with Saudi Arabia were at breaking point owing to the Yemen Civil War. On 11 May, Prime Minister Levi Eshkol warned that Israel would not hesitate to use force on the scale of 7 April if the terrorism along Israel's borders continued unabated. On the

Since the Second Arab-Israeli War of 1956, the United Nations Emergency Force (UNEF) kept an uneasy peace between the Israelis and Arabs along their disputed borders. Here, the commander of UNEF, Major-General Indar Jit Rikhye of the Indian Army (at the front to the immediate right of the three photographers), with a group of his officers inspects a checkpoint between Erez and the Gaza Strip shortly before his troops were withdrawn from the Sinai by the General-Secretary of the UN, U Thant, an action that made war almost inevitable.

same day, the Israeli envoy to the UN, Gideon Rafael, presented a letter to the Security Council reaffirming that Israel would 'act in self-defence as circumstances warrant' under Article 51 of the UN Charter. Two days latter, the Speaker of the Egyptian Parliament, Anwar Sadat, was warned by the Soviet Deputy Foreign Minister, Vladimir Semnov that, according to Soviet military intelligence, up to 11 IDF brigades were concentrating on the Syrian border. The same message was conveyed to President Nasser by the Soviet ambassador in Cairo. Photoreconnaissance flights by the Syrian Air Force and an Egyptian military tour of the border region revealed nothing of the sort. Similarly, the Norwegian General Odd Bull, the commander of the UN Truce Supervision Organization (UNTSO) straddling the border, confirmed this assessment. There were hardly 11 companies of Israeli troops let alone 11 brigades as this would have required the open mobilization of civilian reservists. Nevertheless, the Soviet disinformation was the catalyst for disaster. President Nasser dispatched two divisions across the Suez Canal into the Sinai Peninsula as a show of strength, effectively tripling the number of troops in the area. Since the Sinai was Egyptian territory it did not bother Israel unduly although one IDF reserve brigade was mobilized on 15 May as a precaution. This move by Nasser was calculated to serve two purposes. It showed the Arab world that Egypt was loyal to Syria but without having to deploy combat troops to her northern ally since there was no actual military threat of invasion from the Israelis.

Hysteria swept the Arab world in a renewed wave of anti-Semitism. The imams in the mosques were calling for jihad or holy war against Israel. Troops marching through Cairo on their way to the Sinai chanted 'We are off to Tel Aviv!' Swept up in this tide of euphoria and belligerence, on 16 May, Nasser demanded the withdrawal of the 3,400 troops of the United Nations Emergency Force (UNEF) that had manned the borders between Egypt and Israel since 1957. Unexpectedly, Secretary-General of the United Nations

Arab and Israeli invasion plans

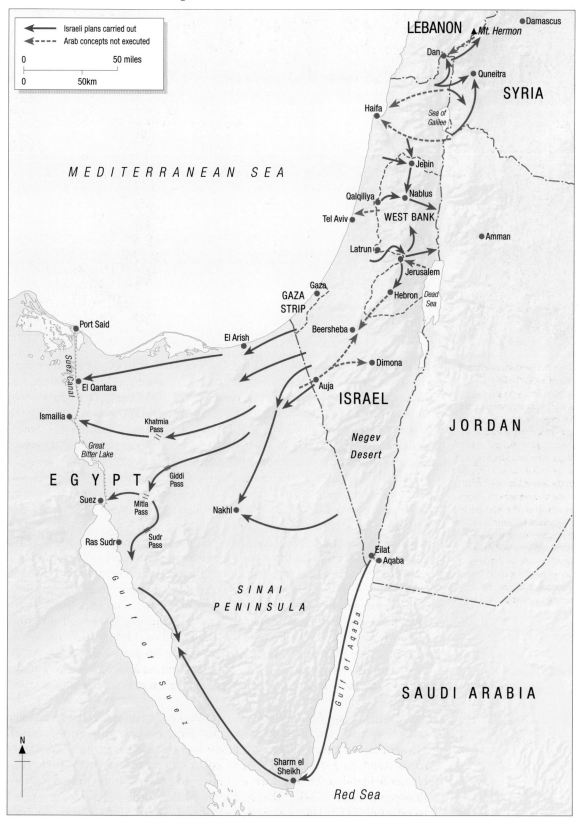

U Thant acceded to the demands without referring the matter either to the General Assembly or the Security Council. It was a colossal blunder that was to haunt U Thant to his dying day. A concerted refusal by the UN would have allowed Nasser to maintain the status quo but now Egyptian and Israeli forces confronted each other toe to toe. It was impossible for President Nasser to back down without huge loss of face in the Arab world. On 20 May, both Israel and Egypt ordered the partial mobilization of their respective reserves while Egyptian units returned from Yemen. With more troops flooding into the Sinai, Egyptian forces occupied positions vacated by the UNEF in Sharm el Sheikh overlooking the Straits of Tiran – Israel's economic jugular vein for her vital oil supplies from Iran. Three days later, Nasser made a bellicose speech to pilots at Bir Gifgafa airbase with the words: 'The armed forces yesterday occupied Sharm el Sheikh ... under no circumstances will we allow the Israeli flag to pass through the Gulf of Aqaba ... if Jews threaten war we tell them "you are welcome, we are ready for war. Our armed forces and all our people are ready for war" ... This water is ours.' It was the action Israel feared the most and the oft-quoted *casus belli* that made war inevitable. Yet Nasser's military aims remained limited with his principal objective being the capture of Eilat and a contiguous border with Jordan: the bitter legacy of the 1948 war. Such a strategy was indicated by the disposition of the Egyptian forces in the Sinai Peninsula.

OPERATION *QAHIR* – *CONQUEROR*

In 1967, the Egyptian Army comprised some 175,000 men. Aside from those forces in Yemen, almost all the combat units of the army were deployed in the Sinai with 18 infantry brigades, one paratroop brigade, six armoured brigades and two mechanized brigades, as well as four Special Forces battalions. These were divided into six divisions. The 20th Palestine Liberation Army Division supported by Egyptian artillery and 50 Sherman tanks was stationed in the Gaza Strip. To the south of the Gaza Strip was the newly formed 7th Infantry Division supported by approximately 100 T-34/85 and IS-3M tanks. Further to the south-east in the Abu Ageila–Quseima area was the 2nd Infantry Division supported by approximately 90 T-34/85 and T-54 tanks. This was considered to be one of the better formations but its commander, Major-General Sadi Naguib, was a political appointee of limited military expertise whose main claim to fame was as a drinking companion of the commander-in-chief of the army, Field Marshal Amer. The 6th Mechanized Division was deployed in the Kuntilla–Nakhl area. It was a good division at full strength with a competent commander, Major-General Abd el Kader Hassan. It in turn was supported by the 1st Armoured Brigade of some 100 T-34/85 and T-54 tanks under the command of Brigadier Hussein Abd al Nataf. In general reserve was the 3rd Infantry Division in the Jebel Libni–Bir Hassna area under the command of another of Field Marshal Amer's cronies, Major-General Osman Nasser. Also in reserve was an armoured task force consisting of 150 T-55 tanks, a paratroop brigade and an artillery brigade under the command of Major-General Saad el Shazli and known as Shazli Force. It was deployed east of Bir Hassna to conduct offensive operations against Eilat and to link up with the Jordanians once war began in a plan codenamed Operation *al-Asad* or *Lion*. In strategic reserve under the control of Field Marshal Amer's GHQ in Cairo was the 4th Armoured Division equipped with 200 modern Soviet T-55 tanks under the command of Major-General Sidki el Ghoul. It was stationed in the central Sinai around Bir Gifgafa. An independent infantry brigade was posted to Sharm el Sheikh overlooking the Straits of Tiran.

In total the Egyptian forces in the Sinai amounted to over 100,000 troops and some 930 tanks. Following standard Soviet doctrine, the divisions were deployed in strongly defended localities of three distinct defensive lines supported by dug-in artillery and armour units. As part of a comprehensive defensive plan codenamed Operation *Qahir* or *Conqueror*, these were to act as a lure to tempt the IDF to attack these 'killing zones' and once the Israeli assault was broken the Egyptian army would move to the offensive. In reality Operation *Qahir* was neither fish nor fowl with the commanders uncertain whether to adopt a defensive or offensive posture. This confusion was compounded by the appointment of General Abd el Mushin Murtagi as the Sinai front commander with his headquarters in Ismailia. Recently returned from undistinguished service in Yemen, he had little knowledge of the Sinai and no rapport with either his divisional commanders or the Sinai field commander, Lieutenant-General Sallah el din Mohsen. The latter demanded clear-cut guidance regarding the true objectives of Operation *Qahir*, but none was forthcoming from either the front HQ at Ismailia or GHQ in Cairo. Indeed, Field Marshal Amer was prone to issuing conflicting orders directly to divisional commanders without consultation with his field and front commanders.

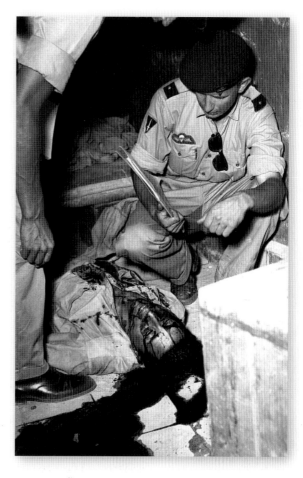

A Belgian officer of 1 Para Commando and his Swedish colleague of UNEF inspect the body of an Israeli agricultural worker killed by fedayeen terrorists from the Gaza Strip. The continuing civilian death toll resulting from terrorist attacks that escalated significantly following the formation of Fatah and the Palestine Liberation Organization was one of the root causes of the Six Day War.

Such confusion percolated down through the ranks. Some units were seriously under strength. Almost a quarter of Egypt's tanks and artillery pieces were unserviceable. Many reservists arrived at the front without uniforms or weapons into a situation of chaos; almost a third never arrived at their assigned positions at all. As a case in point, a newly graduated Egyptian officer, Lieutenant Hamid, was tasked with delivering anti-tank ammunition to Kuntilla. He left on the afternoon of 4 June and bivouacked with his convoy overnight near Nakhl. On the next morning, he reported to the receiving unit at Kuntilla where he was told by a senior officer 'We don't need any ammunition. There isn't going to be a war. Take it back.' The lieutenant rejoined his convoy and started back towards the Suez Canal. Some 30 minutes later, his trucks were being strafed and bombed by the IAF.

ISRAEL – A FAILURE OF DETERRENCE

Confusion reigned on the Israeli side but of a different nature. Initially convinced that there would be no general war in 1967, the Israeli Government was now in the throes of a major crisis. Used to the vituperative rhetoric of Arab leaders, few Israeli politicians believed war was imminent

In the weeks prior to the war, there were deep divisions between the cabinet and the IDF hierarchy bordering on mutiny. It was only with the appointment of former Chief of Staff General Moshe Dayan as Minister of Defense that the IDF gained the leadership it craved, while his return to office boosted Israeli civilian morale as well, thus assuaging both the military and the citizenry at a stroke. With his wide combat experience, he had the strength of character to control the gung-ho IDF whilst imposing a sensible strategy of fighting each Arab country n turn in order to avoid simultaneous warfare on several fronts, hence the priority was defeating Egypt followed by Jordan and finally Syria.

since Nasser had previously deployed divisions into the Sinai in displays of brinkmanship. The closure of the Straits of Tiran on 22 May changed everything in Israeli eyes. Frantic diplomatic efforts were made through the United Nations to bring pressure to bear on the Egyptian Government but to little avail. The United States and Great Britain attempted to form an international naval force, dubbed Operation *Red Sea Regatta*, to force the blockade but it came to naught. By international law, the Israelis were now within their rights to wage war against Egypt but the government demurred. Prime Minister Levi Eshkol still believed that the superpowers could resolve the crisis without armed conflict. A bitter rift grew between the politicians and the generals of the IDF as the situation deteriorated by the day. The damage to the economy following the mobilization of reservists was costing $20 million a day: it was unsustainable even in the short term. Furthermore the existential threat to Israel seemed to be growing greater. On 24 May, Jordan gave permission for Iraqi and Saudi troops to be deployed on her soil. Combat contingents from across the Arab world, from Algeria to Sudan, arrived in Egypt to bolster the forces threatening Israel. Stage by stage, IDF reservists were called to the colours until the factories were virtually empty of able-bodied men, splitting families and raising apprehension across the country. This gradual mobilization made the Eshkol government seem weak compounded by a poorly delivered radio address to the nation by the prime minister that became known as 'the stammering speech' for projecting irresolution. It all came to a head on 30 May. On that day, Jordan and Egypt signed a joint defence pact, albeit with onerous conditions imposed by Nasser including placing the Jordanian armed forces under Egyptian command. The Arab noose around Israel was now complete. Alarm and despondency gripped Israel and civilian morale slumped. Blood transfusion centres sprung up across the country. Public parks and sports stadia were sanctified by rabbis to bury the expected 10,000 dead. Schools and public buildings were converted into makeshift hospitals to house the legions of wounded. Arab leaders continued their poisonous invective while radio stations from Algiers to Baghdad and Cairo to Damascus proclaimed the assured destruction of Israel: 'Arab masses, this is your day. Rush to the battlefield. … Let them know that we shall hang the last imperialist soldier with the entrails of the last Zionist.' Talk of the 'Second Holocaust' became rife. Acutely aware of the Egyptian use of poison gas in Yemen, gas masks were procured in large numbers from America and, ironically, West Germany.

Dayan ex machina

In the IDF, the perspective was very different. Morale among the troops was high and they were champing at the bit for action. Weapons and equipment held in store prior to mobilization had been readied and were in place on the borders. The forces were deployed in accordance with the operational plan codenamed *Sadan*. This was essentially defensive in posture but allowed the IDF to switch rapidly to the offensive. By the end of May, offensive plans had been finalized by Major-General Yitzhak Rabin, the IDF Chief of Staff, and Brigadier-General Yeshayahu Gavish, GOC Southern Command, with the intention of destroying the Egyptian forces in the Sinai so that Israel would then be in a position to advance to the Suez Canal. The overall plan to achieve this aim was divided into four phases, the first of which – the 'breakthrough' phase – called for the rupture of the first Egyptian line in two places: firstly in the Rafah–El Arish sector by an *ugda* commanded by Brigadier-General

Prior to the war, relations between Prime Minister Levi Eshkol and his Chief of Staff, Maj. Gen. Yitzhak Rabin, became increasingly strained, shown here in the centre of the photo flanked by Brig. Gen. Israel Tal, commander of the IAC, and Brig. Gen. Chaim Bar Lev, the Deputy Chief of Staff.

Israel Tal and secondly in the Um Katef–Abu Ageila sector by another *ugda* commanded by Brigadier-General Ariel Sharon. Once these breakthroughs had been achieved then the second phase would see the second Egyptian line penetrated and their armoured reserves in this line, destroyed. This second phase required a third *ugda*, commanded by Brigadier-General Avraham Yoffe, to make a deep penetration through the virtually trackless sand dunes to join up with the others. The third phase would then follow and called for the complete rout of the main Egyptian armoured forces – the long-ranging tentacles of Sharon's force constantly harrying the retreating Egyptians, whilst Yoffe's *ugda* blocked the Mitla and Giddi passes, and Tal's destroyed the concentrations of enemy armour in the Bir Gifgafa area. Once these battles were completed then the way to the Suez Canal would be clear. While the attack was developing in the Sinai other Israeli troops, mainly infantry, but including the 8th Armored Brigade, covered Eilat and were to be deployed in the regions of Mitzpeh Ramon, Nitzana, and along the Gaza Strip. However, the whole success of the offensive was predicated on an overwhelming pre-emptive strike by the IAF to destroy the Egyptian Air Force and gain air supremacy.

Following the disastrous 'stammering speech', the IDF high command demanded a meeting with the Prime Minister and his cabinet. The radio address had severely affected the morale of the troops stationed in the heat of the Negev Desert, who were waiting fervently for a decision. In a fierce confrontation, the general staff claimed that the state's very existence was at stake unless the IDF acted immediately. In highly emotive terms, Brigadier-General Sharon berated Eshkol with the words 'Inaction on our part shows powerlessness. We're making ourselves look like an empty vessel, a desperate state. We've never before been so humiliated. Your hesitation will cost thousands of lives.' Under such intense pressure, Prime Minister Levi Eshkol felt compelled to relinquish his role as Minister of Defense and offer the post to General Moshe Dayan; an iconic military figure who represented true resilience and fortitude in the eyes of the Israeli people rather than the weakness of civilian politicians. At the same time, a government of national unity was formed with opposition leader, Menachem Begin, becoming a

TOP

In the weeks before the Six Day War, many Israelis lived in mortal fear of annihilation as the bellicose and vitriolic rhetoric of the Arab world intensified. Extensive civil defence exercises were conducted to protect the civilian population against the prospect of air attack from Arab air forces. Here, nurses usher their charges into an underground shelter at the Kibbutz Nahal Oz near the town of Sderot and in close proximity to the Gaza Strip.

BOTTOM

Schoolchildren in Tel Aviv are instructed in the rudiments of first aid in the days leading up to the war. Such was the expectation of significant civilian casualties that many schools were converted into makeshift hospitals. Even sports stadia and public parks were sanctified by the chief rabbinate as potential mass burial grounds for the victims of indiscriminate air attacks.

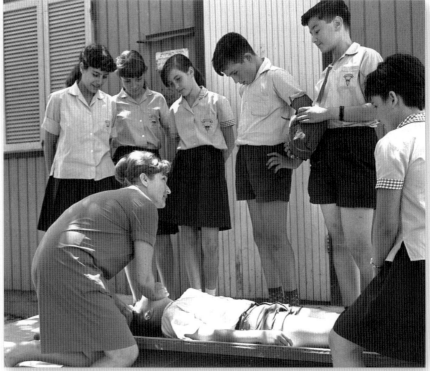

minister without portfolio. On 2 June, Dayan scrutinized the war plans with the practised eye of a soldier and a politician. Israel's original war aims were confined solely to defeating Egypt despite the fact that Syria had been the root cause of the confrontation. Jordan had been informed that if she remained on the sidelines the country would not be attacked. Dayan made three fundamental alterations to the overall plans. Firstly, he insisted that a joint army/navy task force should capture Sharm el Sheikh and thus open the

Straits of Tiran: the original *casus belli* as proclaimed by Israel. Secondly, he explicitly forbade the planned occupation of the Gaza Strip, stating with great prescience that Gaza 'bristled with problems … a nest of wasps' and it would be lunacy to be 'stuck with a quarter of a million Palestinians'. Thirdly, with equal prescience, Dayan ordered that Israeli forces should not occupy the east bank of the Suez Canal since this would mean the closing of the international waterway and give Nasser no alternative but to continue the conflict. Israeli troops were to halt ten kilometres (six miles) from the canal. The revised plan was now codenamed *Nachshonim*.

It was presented to the cabinet that night. Once more the general staff demanded immediate resolution. Yet Eshkol did not let slip the dogs of war until a final flurry of diplomatic trips was undertaken to garner international support. For Israel, the urbane and eloquent Foreign Minister, Abba Eban, and the head of Mossad, Meir Amit, were dispatched to Washington DC to consult Capitol Hill and the CIA respectively. While cautioned by the US not to precipitate military action, President Lyndon Johnson made the Delphic statement to Eban 'Israel will not be alone unless it decides to go it alone.' Thanks to a CIA assessment, the President added 'All of our intelligence people are unanimous that if the UAR [Egypt] attacks, you will whip hell out of them.' After meetings with Secretary of State Dean Rusk and Secretary of Defense Robert McNamara, as well as James Angleton of the CIA, Amit returned to Tel Aviv with an 'amber light' for an Israeli pre-emptive strike. In Amit's report to the new government of national unity, the colour of the light took on a greenish hue. It was sufficient. The cabinet decided on war. Only the date remained undetermined. Abba Eban cautioned that in the event of war, Israel would have but a few days, probably three, before international pressure brought a ceasefire. Conversely, Egyptian efforts to elicit Soviet diplomatic support failed entirely. Having instigated the crisis in the first place, the Soviet Union explicitly denied Egypt the opportunity to open hostilities and thus gain the undoubted advantages of a pre-emptive strike. Only if Egypt were attacked would Soviet diplomatic and *matériel* support be forthcoming. The initiative now passed irrevocably to Israel. On 4 June, the Israeli cabinet finally acquiesced to immediate military action following the endorsement of Maj. Gen. Rabin 'Never has the IDF been more ready and more prepared for war.' To many in the IDF and indeed to some western intelligence services, the assessment by Brigadier-General Uzi Narkiss, GOC Central Command, of Arab capabilities rang true 'They're a bubble of soap and with one pinprick they'll burst.' And the pinprick came in the shape of the pitot tube of a Mirage IIICJ fighter-bomber.

OPPOSING COMMANDERS

ISRAELI COMMANDERS

As of 5 June 1967, the IDF possessed a formidable array of talent across the ranks of all three services although the Israeli Navy did not enjoy the same level of resources as the army or air force. Most had served in the two previous wars and all had extensive combat experience. Their influence over the political decision-making process was highly significant in the timing and prosecution of the war.

In overall command was the mercurial and charismatic **General Moshe Dayan** as Minister of Defense. As Chief of Staff of the IDF, he had orchestrated the emphatic Israeli victory in the Sinai Campaign of 1956. Although retired from the IDF, he was appointed as Minister of Defense on 2 June as the crisis facing Israel deepened. Throughout the war, his instincts were remarkable at the strategic and operational planning levels but his innate pessimism often meant that he did not impose his will fully upon his impetuous subordinates.

The Chief of Staff of the IDF was the shy but abrasive **Major-General Yitzhak Rabin**. A native-born Israeli, he had seen heavy fighting during the War of Independence on the Burma Road in the battle for Jerusalem as commander of the elite Harel Brigade. Despite the best efforts of his troops, the Old City was

The three top military officers of the IDF confer at the Kirya General Headquarters (GHQ) in Tel Aviv on 3 June 1967. In the middle is Chief of Staff Maj. Gen. Yitzhak Rabin with his deputy Brig. Gen. Chaim Bar Lev to the left and former IAF commander, Brig. Gen. Ezer Weizmann, the Chief of Operations on the right.

denied to the Israelis; a matter that he rectified some 20 years later. By the end of the war he was Chief of Operations for the Southern Front. He then became GOC of Northern Command where he adopted an aggressive posture against the Syrians over the disputed Demilitarized Zones and the diversion of the Jordan River headwaters culminating in the Water War of 1965/66. In 1964, Rabin was appointed as IDF Chief of Staff when he oversaw a significant expansion of the IAF and the Israeli Armored Corps (IAC). In 1966, Prime Minster Levi Eshkol asked him to serve a second term as IDF Chief of Staff. Previously, Eshkol and Rabin enjoyed a successful working relationship but as the crisis mounted in early 1967 it became distinctly problematical leading to serious divisions between the IDF and the government. Indeed, in the days just prior to the war of June 1967, Yitzhak Rabin suffered a 'nervous collapse' for a couple of days due it was said to days of lack of food with an over-reliance on nicotine and black coffee. During this time, the IDF Chief of the General Staff Operations Branch, Brigadier-General Ezer Weizman, formerly commander of the IAF, fulfilled his duties.

From 27 April 1966, the *Chel Ha'Avir* or IAF was commanded by **Brigadier-General Mordechai 'Motti' Hod**. An intense, demonstrative man, Hod was a consummate professional with wide experience of jet aircraft. For years he had been refining the plans for a pre-emptive aerial strike against Israel's Arab neighbours as well as maintaining air supremacy over the country against any foreign incursion. The whole success of the IDF operational plan for the coming war depended on the IAF and its personnel so a huge responsibility lay with generals Hod and Weizman.

In overall command of the Israeli forces on the Sinai front since 1965 was **Brigadier-General Yeshayahu Gavish** as GOC Southern Command. He had made extensive studies of Soviet military doctrine and devised his operational plans to defeat the Egyptian forces in their defensive localities accordingly. For this purpose, he had three *ugdas* or divisional-sized formations, each with highly experienced commanders.

On the northern axis was Ugda Tal of **Brigadier-General Israel Tal**, the commander of the IAC. A strict disciplinarian in an otherwise casual army, the diminutive Talik had created a powerful armoured force – the 'mailed fists' or

LEFT
The Deputy Chief of Staff, Brig. Gen. Chaim Bar Lev greets Brig. Gen. Avraham Yoffe (left) during a briefing in the Sinai. A few weeks prior to the war Yoffe was summoned to see the GOC Southern Command, Brig. Gen. Gavish. As the director of Israel's Nature Protection Society, Yoffe was wearing civilian clothes for what he assumed was a courtesy call. He left the meeting in a brigadier-general's uniform with the command of the 31st Reserve Armored Division.

RIGHT
With the winged cobra insignia of the Paratroop Command on his shoulder, Col. Rafael Eitan confers with a subordinate officer during the battle of Rafah Junction. Later in the war, 'Raful' Eitan was severely wounded in the head. During his distinguished military career, he led many Special Forces operations, including the capture of Adolf Eichmann, and found lasting fame when he commanded the Israeli forces on the Golan in the opening days of the October War of 1973. He subsequently became the Chief of Staff of the IDF.

Egrofei Shiryon that were to be at the forefront of all the land campaigns of the war. Ugda Tal comprised three brigades with 250 tanks and 50 artillery pieces.

On the central axis was Ugda Yoffe composed of reservists under the command of **Brigadier-General (Res) Avraham Yoffe.** Born in 1913, Yoffe joined the Haganah, forerunner of the IDF at the age of 16. After serving in the British Army during World War II, he was a battalion commander during the War of Independence. During the Sinai Campaign of 1956, he commanded the 9th Brigade that captured Sharm el Sheikh. After the war he became GOC Southern Command and therefore knew the terrain intimately when he returned as a reservist general to command Ugda Yoffe. It comprised two brigades.

Facing the formidable defended locality of Abu Ageila and Um Katef was Ugda Sharon under the command of **Brigadier-General Ariel Sharon.** A legendary figure in the IDF, Sharon was a hard-driving paratrooper who had led many punitive raids against the fedayeen. In the Sinai Campaign of 1956, his paratroop brigade captured the strategic Mitla Pass but at such a cost that it hindered his career until Maj. Gen. Rabin became chief of staff in 1964. Thereafter, he became Infantry School Commander and Head of Army Training Branch before receiving a combined-arms *ugda* in the Sinai. Ugda Sharon comprised four brigades.

Even at brigade level, the IDF commanders were outstanding with paratroop officers such as colonels **Rafael Eitan** and **Dani Matt**; armour officers such as colonels **Shumel Gonen** and **Albert Mendler** and infantry officers such as colonels **Yekutiel Adam** and **Yehuda Reshef**. Throughout the IDF, initiative was encouraged in all ranks to maintain the momentum of the offensive. This was imbued in the officer corps and junior leaders in the ethos of '*Aharai*' – 'Follow me!' From the earliest days, Israel lacked strategic depth whereby it could defend its borders. IDF doctrine demanded that the battle be taken into enemy territory to minimize the threat to Israel's population centres that lay so close to its frontiers and often within artillery range of its enemies. In the words of Gen. Moshe Dayan 'Aggression was in the army's bones and spirit.'

EGYPTIAN COMMANDERS

This was certainly not the case in the Egyptian armed forces. Initiative and aggression were not seen as virtues at all as this might reflect on the inactivity and ineptitude of senior officers. Advancement relied on patronage and the more senior the appointment, the more this was crucial in a Byzantine world of cronyism and power cliques. The profession of arms was of subsidiary importance.

The supreme head of the Egyptian Armed Forces was notionally **President Gamal Abd el Nasser** who had come to power in a revolution orchestrated by a clique known as the Free Officers Movement. Although the armed forces acted as the guarantor of government stability, there was no actual political control over them. Prior to 1967, there was no written constitutional basis for national defence or a national security policy. Equally, the responsibilities of the President, Defence Minister and the Chief of Staff of the Armed Forces were not delineated or their relationship to one another formally determined particularly during times of crisis. In fact the armed forces were not monitored by any government body be it parliament or the council of ministers, let alone a free press. Accordingly, the command and control of the Egyptian Army was

Field Marshal Abd el Hakim Amer exhorts his troops before a coterie of high-ranking officers of the Egyptian armed forces. Almost without exception, they proved to be utterly incompetent during the war and the real architects of their own defeat. On 14 September 1967, the disgraced Amer was given the choice of being tried for high treason, with the inevitability of conviction and execution, or dying by his own hand. He chose death by poison, although some accounts indicate that he may well have been assisted in his demise by Nasser's henchmen. He received a state funeral with full military honours.

the preserve of one man, **Field Marshal Abd el Hakim Amer**. As a major in the Free Officers Movement in 1952, he was a friend and crony of Colonel Nasser. Thereafter, Amer enjoyed possibly the most meteoric rise in rank in the annals of military history climbing from major to field marshal in just six years. Despite failures in the Yemen civil war and as overall commander of the forces of the abortive United Arab Republic with Syria, Nasser remained loyal to his crony and even made him Vice President and Deputy Supreme Commander in 1964, and therefore heir presumptive to Nasser himself. More disastrously, Nasser never acquainted himself with the real state of the armed forces before he embarked on his strategy of brinkmanship in early 1967. Thanks to the blandishments of Field Marshal Amer, he convinced himself that Egypt could now defeat Israel since it no longer had the support of Britain and France as it had in 1956.

Another critical failure was the complete lack of communication and co-ordination between the army and the other two services, the navy and air force. There was no joint body to conduct joint operations or to incorporate the various branches of the army and air force into an integrated air defence system. This should have been the role of the Chief of Staff of the Armed Forces, **Lieutenant-General Anwar al Khadi**, but each service jealously guarded its independence. Equally extraordinary is the fact that both the commanders of the Egyptian Air Force, **General Mohammed Sidqi Mahmoud**, and the Egyptian Navy, **Admiral Soliman Ezzat**, were the same men that had failed so dismally during the Second Arab-Israeli War of 1956 when the air force was destroyed on the ground and the navy never left port. Field Marshal Amer of course was in command of the army during 1956 as well.

As noted above the profession of arms often remained secondary in the lives of many senior officers. As a case in point, Amer was also the chairman of the High Dam Authority, chairman of the Public Transportation Authority and chairman of the Committees for the Liquidation of Feudalism. For other officers, one of their more diverting tasks was as secretaries to the various sporting clubs dotted along the Nile River. This ordinarily entailed finishing one's military duties on a Thursday afternoon and not returning until Tuesday: this habit continued even when units were deployed to the Sinai in May 1967. One such club secretary was **General Abd el Mushin Murtagi**. As a crony of

Army reservists congregate at a base of IDF Southern Command just prior to the war. The IDF had a highly efficient mobilization plan that allowed full mobilization within days. However, these troops could not be massed on the borders for any prolonged length of time owing to the resulting damage to the economy. It was a prime reason for Israel deciding on a pre-emptive strike against Egypt.

Amer, he was appointed as commander-in-chief of the Sinai Front on 15 May 1967 having just returned from Yemen where he had acted as the senior Political Commissar. He therefore had no knowledge of the Sinai or his subordinate commanders and he inherited the *Qahir* operational plan that had been in place since the year before. However, Murtagui was one of Amer's close drinking companions, as were several divisional commanders in the Sinai – a rather dubious qualification for high rank with the country on the verge of war. Needless to say there were many highly competent and committed officers in the Egyptian armed forces but they were not best served by a corrupt and inept high command. And so it proved in battle.

But possibly the greatest failure for the Egyptian armed forces was in the field of military intelligence. Whereas the Israeli intelligence agencies knew the location of every Egyptian aircraft at every Egyptian air base, the Egyptians knew nothing about Israeli dispositions and capabilities. In Egypt, military intelligence was an organ of a repressive, autocratic state whose role was to root out dissent within the armed forces rather than providing them with vital facts and figures about the potential enemy. As **Air Vice Marshal Abd el-Hamid El-Dighidi** later commented ruefully 'Egyptian military intelligence was spying on me, not for me.'

OPPOSING FORCES

Women have always played an important part in the activities of the IDF from the earliest days of the Palmach. Dappled beneath a camouflage net, a female soldier maintains communications at a formation headquarters deep in the Sinai Desert.

Superficially the forces of the Arab world arraigned against Israel seemed overwhelming as the figures below indicate. Although Israel managed successfully to portray herself to the world as David standing alone against a monolithic Arab Goliath, the reality was different. Despite their numbers, the Arab armies were riven by operational and doctrinal difficulties, with virtually no political or military cooperation at any level between the various countries. There was no common plan to invade Israel in a coordinated campaign. After the destruction of their respective air forces on the opening day of the war, Egypt, Jordan and Syria stood passively on the defensive as each army was destroyed by the IDF in turn, with Iraq and other Arab military contingents posturing impotently on the sidelines. All the while the peoples of the Arab world were fed the most monstrous lies about the conduct of the war that made the abject defeat all the more bitter to bear.

	Israel	Arabs	Egypt	Jordan	Syria	Iraq
Manpower	250,000	328,000	210,000	55,000	63,000	
Brigades	25	4~~2~~4	22	10	12	
Artillery	745	~~960~~ 1153	575	263	315	
Tanks	1,294*	2,33~~0~~8	1,300	288	750	
APCs	2,000	1,845	1,050	210	585	
SAMs	50	160	0	0	0	
AAA	550	~~2,000~~+ 93	950	143	1,000	
Aircraft	286**	692	431	28	127	106

* The total included 522 Shermans; 184 AMX-13s; 250 M48 Pattons and 338 Centurions. The APCs were all World War II vintage M3 half-tracks.

** 196 of these were front-line strike aircraft.

ISRAELI FORCES

On full mobilization, the Israeli Army comprised some 250,000 men of whom almost three-quarters were reservists and one-quarter conscripts, leavened by several thousand professional soldiers. Male conscripts served for two and a half years and women for two, usually between the ages of 18 and 21. Men then served in the reserves up to the age of 50 for a month of training annually or on operational duty should the need arise. Out of its 25 brigades, nine were armoured, two were fully mechanized and ten were infantry, some partly mechanized, as well as four paratroop brigades which also acted as elite assault troops. Each brigade comprised some 4,500 men depending on its specific role.

The brigades were assigned to six *ugdas*, or division-size task forces, whose composition varied according to their assigned mission and geographical area. Note that the composition of each of the three *ugdas* of Southern Command in June 1967 was different. Of the nine brigades in Southern Command, five were armoured, three were mechanized/motorized infantry and one consisted of paratroops in a mechanized role. In addition there were three brigades as an operational reserve, one armoured and two infantry. In total, Southern Command had 70,000 troops and approximately 800 tanks with nearly all of the most modern types in the IAC inventory. The Israeli Army was well motivated since many believed that the very existence of Israel was at stake but much of its equipment was of World War II vintage. Furthermore its operational doctrine was little different from that of the Wehrmacht at the outset of the battle of France in 1940. However, it had invested heavily in modern communications equipment that allowed for a flexible command and control system: a structure that suited the Israeli temperament with all levels of command being able to display initiative in any overall offensive plan from an infantry company to an armoured brigade.

EGYPTIAN FORCES

Of its official strength of 210,000 men in June 1967, the Egyptian Army had some 100,000 troops in the Sinai Peninsula and approximately 50,000 in Yemen with the remainder stationed to the west of the Suez Canal to protect Cairo. The Sinai Front Command comprised some six divisions with 930 tanks, 200 assault guns and 900 artillery pieces – a formidable force by any standards They were deployed in separate heavily defended localities as part of Operation *Qahir*. However these positions were not mutually supportive and had been starved of funds since the bulk of the Egyptian military operational budget had been committed to the forces in Yemen for several years. The army was comprised of professional soldiers leavened with a large proportion of conscripts undergoing three years of national service. As a regular force it was able to stay for long periods in its prepared positions in the Sinai, a situation that the IDF could not endure owing to the damage to the economy of prolonged mobilization. Accordingly, the Egyptians tended to be defensive in nature compounded by inadequate training and a lack of mechanization among its infantry units. The fundamental flaw in the Egyptian Army lay in its officer corps, which was heavily politicized with senior commanders beholden to either Amer or Nasser, whose respective adherents were mutually antagonistic and therefore detrimental to the standards of a professional army. As to the individual common soldier he was of a stoical disposition and grateful for regular meals and whatever rudimentary medical services there were, although Egyptian officers showed scant regard for the welfare of their troops. The command structure was rigid and allowed little initiative to regimental officers. More damaging was the persistent lack of communications between divisional commanders and their brigades leading to a chronic inability to react to developments on the battlefield, whether from higher command or by enemy actions. This problem was due in large part to the complete lack of field training exercises for large formations: the last major divisional exercise conducted by the Egyptian army codenamed *Ishtar* occurred in 1954. The only regular large-scale military activities were the annual parades in Cairo to celebrate the revolution of 1952. It was not an operational doctrine to guarantee success against the IDF.

ORDERS OF BATTLE

ISRAELI ORDER OF BATTLE – SOUTHERN COMMAND

GOC	Brig. Gen. Yeshayahu Gavish
84th Armored Division	Brig. Gen. Israel 'Talik' Tal
7th Armored Brigade	Col. Shumel Gonen (88 Centurion & 66 Patton)
60th Armored Brigade	Col. Menachem Aviram (86 Sherman & AMX-13)
202nd Paratroop Brigade	Col. Rafael 'Raful' Eitan
Recce Task Force	Col. Uri Baron
Granit Task Force	Col. Yisrael Granit
46th Tank Battalion	Lt. Col. Uri Bar-On
215th Artillery Regiment	
31st Armored Division	Brig. Gen. Avraham Yoffe
200th Armored Brigade	Col. Yissacher 'Isska' Shadmi
520th Armored Brigade	Col. Elhanan Sela
38th Armored Division	Brig. Gen. Ariel 'Arik' Sharon
14th Armored Brigade	Col. Mordechai Zippori
99th Infantry Brigade	Col. Yekutiel 'Kuti' Adam
80th Paratroop Brigade	Col. Dani Matt
214th Artillery Regiment	
226th Tank Batalion	
35th Paratroop Brigade	Col. Aharon Davidi
8th Armored Brigade (Ind)	Col. Avraham 'Albert' Mandler *
40th Artilery Battalion	
11th Infantry Brigade (Ind)	Col. Yehuda Reshef
55th Paratroop Brigade	Col. Mordechai 'Motti' Gur **

* Reassigned to Northern Command
**Reassigned to Central Command

EGYPTIAN ORDER OF BATTLE – SINAI FRONT COMMAND

Front commander	Gen. Abd el Mushin Murtagi
Field commander	Lt. Gen. Sallah el din Mohsen
2nd Infantry Division	Maj. Gen. Sadi Naguib
3rd Infantry Division	Maj. Gen. Osman Nasser
4th Armoured Division	Maj. Gen. Sidki el Ghoul
Task Force Shazli	Maj. Gen. Saad el Shazli
6th Mechanized Division	Maj. Gen. Abd el Kader Hassan
7th Infantry Division	Maj. Gen. Abd el Aziz Soliman
20th PLA Division Gaza	Maj. Gen. Mohammed Abd el Moneim Hasni
Infantry Brigade (Ind)	Brig. Mohammed Abd el Moneim Khalil
1st Armoured Brigade	Brig. Hussein Abd el Nataf
125th Armoured Brigade	Brig. Ahmed El-Naby

OPERATION *MOKED*

AIR FRANCE

As commander of the IAF, Brig. Gen. Mordechai 'Motti' Hod keeps his hand in as a pilot at the controls of a Mirage IIICJ. Operation *Moked* was the result of 12 years of planning and many months of concerted practice against mock-ups of Egyptian airbases hidden in the Negev Desert. As the architect of Operation *Moked*, Hod was convinced that it was a war-winning strategy.

During the War of Independence, the *Sherut Avir* or Aviation Service of the Haganah flew a motley collection of light aircraft configured for photo-reconnaissance and even as primitive bombers. On 27 May 1948, the *Chel Ha'Avir* or Israel Defense Forces/Air Force (IAF) was formed. Thereafter it had to beg, borrow and steal suitable aircraft from around the world in a series of often covert and dubious acquisition deals. Clandestine operations such as *Balak* and *Velvetta* procured Messerschmitt Bf-109s (Mezeks) from Czechoslovakia, B-17 Flying Fortresses from scrapyards in Florida, Spitfires from France as well as Beaufighters, Harvards, Mosquitos, Mustangs, Hudsons, Dakotas and a host of other types – most leaving various countries with spurious flight plans that tended to end up at Dov, Ekron or Ramat David air force bases in Israel. The principal IDF strike aircraft during the early 1950s was the de Havilland DH 98 Mosquito FB6 but when the Egyptian Air Force was equipped with the Soviet MiG-15 jet fighter from 1954 onwards, urgent replacements were required for both air defence and close air support. Under the dynamic leadership of Major-General Dan Tolkovski, a former Royal Air Force officer, the IAF rapidly re-equipped with jet aircraft; the first being the Gloster Meteor F8, soon followed by the NF13 model with its airborne interception radar to give an all-weather and night-fighter capability. In August 1955, Col. Nasser concluded a massive arms deal with the Soviet Union. Within a short period, the Egyptian Air Force was equipped with a modern all jet, both fighter and bomber, force capable of striking multiple targets in Israel from extensive airbases recently evacuated by the British following their departure from the Suez Canal Zone. To counter the MiG-15, the IAF procured the French multi-role Dassault Ouragan and the Sud Aviation Vautour, followed by the far more capable Dassault Mystère IVA fighter from early 1956. On 1 September 1955, the first aerial combat between Egyptian and Israeli jets occurred when an Israeli Meteor shot down two Egyptian Vampires. Another Vampire was shot down by a Dassault Ouragan on 12 April 1956. Within months the Second Arab-Israeli War erupted with Israel fighting in conjunction with the British and French to re-establish international control over the Suez Canal. The Anglo-French invasion of the Canal Zone was preceded by an extensive air campaign that effectively destroyed the Egyptian Air Force on the ground, although some aircraft sought sanctuary in Syria and Saudi Arabia. It was the precursor for Operation *Moked* in 1967.

The backbone of the IAF during the Six Day War was the several types of French-designed aircraft, with those shown here including a flight of four Fouga Magister training aircraft leading the Dassault Ouragan fighter-bomber (left); Dassault Super Mystère B.2 fighter (right) with the Sud Aviation Vautour II light bomber to the rear.

While the procurement of more modern aircraft proceeded apace, Maj. Gen. Tolkovski implemented a policy that largely pertains to this day. Realizing that the joint Arab air forces would always enjoy a marked numerical superiority in aircraft, he emphasized the need for qualitative superiority through rigorous and continuous training. Furthermore, Israel's geographical position surrounded by potential enemies at close quarters precluded the luxury of a strategic bomber force since close air support of the ground forces was a primary requirement. Similarly a pure air superiority fighter was a luxury the IDF could ill afford. Accordingly, multi-purpose fighter-bombers capable of fulfilling both roles became a priority. Fortuitously, Israel enjoyed close ties with France, based on mutual hostility towards Nasser who was supporting FLN revolutionaries in the French colony of Algeria. Furthermore, Israel's participation in the Anglo-French attempt to regain control of the Suez Canal was rewarded with the provision of a French nuclear reactor that was built at Dimona in the Negev Desert in 1957. It was a significant escalation in the Arab-Israeli arms race. In the same year, Brigadier-General Ezer Weizman became commander of the IAF. From the outset, he was convinced that in any coming war the foremost role of the IAF would be a pre-emptive strike against the Arab air forces yet the IDF General Staff remained unconvinced by Weizman's Operation *Moked* or *Focus*. In reality, more capable aircraft were necessary to implement the plan. They arrived in the shape of the Dassault Mirage IIIC in a hugely expensive $200 million procurement package for 76 models of a special variant designated Mirage IIICJ – the J meaning *juif* or Jew in French. In Israeli service it was known as *Shahak* or Skyblazer. The principal difference of this variant was the fitting of twin DEFA 552 30mm cannons and under-wing pylons for more ordnance in the ground attack role. In addition, the IAF developed a special rocket-powered bomb for the destruction of concrete runways. The technology for Operation *Moked* was now in place. However, the human element was just

With its pitot tube shown to advantage, a Mirage IIIC displays the various sorts of ordnance it was able to deliver including a general-purpose 400kg (882-pound) bomb (left) next to which is a Matra launcher with 68mm SNEB Free Flight Aerial Rockets (FFAR). In the foreground are the heavier T-10 120mm FFAR. Note that the military censor has obliterated the squadron insignia and aircraft number on the tail fin.

as important. Throughout the 1960s, the plan was refined and perfected thanks to constant practice by aircrews and superb military intelligence gathering by Mossad and Shin Bet that provided the very latest information about Egyptian aircraft deployments and even details of individual pilots. Mock-ups of Egyptian airbases were constructed in the Negev Desert. They were attacked repeatedly in multiple passes until the geography of each and every airfield was imprinted in the minds of pilots and aircrew. Furthermore, the IAF achieved a considerable force multiplier whereby each combat aircraft could be refuelled and rearmed in a remarkable turnaround rate of less than ten minutes to allow anything up to eight missions a day to be flown at a sustained rate for several days. This was due in part to the fact that the IAF had at least three trained pilots for each front-line aircraft. Whereas IAF aircraft availability was in the high 90 per cent rate, the Egyptian Air Force was lucky to achieve 30 per cent. By June 1967, the IAF was almost exclusively equipped with French-designed aircraft hence its nickname of 'Air France'. It had honed its skills in ground-attack missions, both against air bases and in support of ground troops, to a remarkable degree. Day in and day out, IAF fighter-bombers took off at dawn and flew out over the Mediterranean Sea on combat patrols, dropping to sea level to avoid radar detection before returning to land. Day in and day out, Egyptian, Jordanian and Syrian radar sites tracked these flights with monotonous regularity. As dawn rose on 5 June 1967, it was like any other day except just hours before their routine take-offs the pilots of the *Chel Ha'Avir* were briefed for multiple combat missions using virtually every strike aircraft in the IAF inventory: 196 in all. Operation *Moked* had begun.

DO IT RIGHT

In his order of the day, Brig. Gen. Mordechai Hod pronounced 'The spirit of Israel's heroes accompanies us to battle. … From Joshua Bin-Nun, King David, the Maccabees and the fighters of 1948 and 1956, we shall draw the strength and courage to strike the Egyptians who threaten our safety, our independence and our future. Fly, soar at the enemy, destroy him and scatter him in the desert so that the people of Israel may live secure on their land for generations.' One squadron commander told his pilots moments before Operation *Moked* began 'With you in the cockpit sit the People of Israel, generations of Jews, and each one of them is confident that you will do it right.' At 0710hrs, 16 Magister Fouga jet trainers took off in a routine patrol pattern using radio frequencies normally used by Mirage and Mystère fighters as a subterfuge. Between 0714 and 0730hrs, a further 183 aircraft took to the air from bases all over Israel – some 95 per cent of the IAF's front-line strength. Just 12 fighters remained on stand by or in the air over Israel to defend its airspace against attack. Just one aircraft was declared unserviceable. As usual most of the aircraft turned westwards towards the Mediterranean Sea. As usual they were tracked by the sophisticated British-manufactured radar system at Ajlun in Jordan. However, the Jordanian operators immediately realized that the scale of the flights was far different from normal. The duty officer quickly radioed the codeword *Inab* or grape in Arabic as a warning of impending attack to the Egyptian Defence Minister in Cairo. It was to no avail. On the previous day, the Egyptians had changed the radio codes without informing the Jordanians so the message was now indecipherable. After flying westwards for 18 minutes at wave-top height, the air armada turned southwards in total radio silence. The aircraft flew at an altitude rarely above 18m (60ft). One pilot of 101 Squadron recalled:

> We were flying low and fast over a blue desert with nothing to hang onto for identification. I was very tense, waiting for the moment when we had to turn south. We turned. The route we were on took us in towards the Nile Delta. We passed over some fishing boats but the fishermen didn't even bother to lift their heads. Then ahead of us, I saw the golden strip of sand on the edge of Lake Bardawill in Sinai. This was the spot where we were supposed to cross.

This gun camera view shows the initial attack by *Shahaks* of No. 101 Squadron against Ilyushin Il-28 medium bombers at the Egyptian airbase at Cairo West. Having taken off at 0717hrs on 5 June 1967, the three Mirage IIICJ fighter bombers, callsign Vilon or Curtain, struck Cairo West at 0750hrs. In a series of devastating strafing passes, eight Tupolev Tu-16, three Ilyushin Il-28 and three MiG-21 aircraft were destroyed.

In the classic 'finger-four' formation, a flight of Mirage IIICJ *Shahak* fighters of No. 101 Squadron, with tail numbers 09, 42, 51 and 52, conduct a routine patrol over the Jezreel Valley in the heartland of Israel in March 1967. During the Six Day War, No. 101 Squadron flew 337 sorties at an average of 56 sorties a day with just over 11 sorties per pilot or almost two sorties per pilot per day. The sorties were split more or less equally between air combat and ground attack missions. The squadron was credited with 14 air-to-air victories with a kill-to-loss ratio of seven-to-one. Of these four aircraft, *Shahak* 09 was destroyed a MiG-19 by cannon fire on 7 June 1967.

The lake was chock full of fishing boats and fishermen and I remember that this time they looked up and waved as we flew by. Naturally they had no idea as to who we were or where we were going. A few seconds later we could see the Suez Canal. The scenery below changed. Now it was green and cultivated as we approached the Nile Delta and Cairo West [airbase].

Back in Tel Aviv, the IDF High Command was clustered in the underground command bunker of the Kyria known as the HaBor or Pit. Among them were generals Dayan, Rabin, Weizman and Hod, all anxiously waiting for news of the air operation. The whole outcome of the war depended on Operation *Moked*. Its concept was simple – the destruction of the Egyptian Air Force on the ground. Its execution was anything but simple. It required a simultaneous attack on 10 Egyptian airbases, followed by 14 others, by aircraft of varying speeds and capabilities carrying different ordnance. 'The suspense was incredible,' Ezer Weizman recounted, 'for five years I had been talking of this operation, explaining it, hatching it, dreaming of it, manufacturing it link by link, training men to carry it out. Now in another quarter of an hour, we would know if it was only a dream or whether it would come true.' His successor as commander of the IAF, Brig. Gen. Hod had been equally involved in the gestation of Operation *Moked* but he had every confidence as he sat impassively, drinking draft after draft of water. Few ministers knew anything about the plan and even IDF commanders were given but the shortest of briefings on the subject. A key factor to success or failure was the unconventional timing of the attack. Rather than attacking at dawn, the IAF decided to wait for a couple of hours until 0745hrs, 0845hrs Egyptian time. By this time, the morning mists over the Nile Delta had dispersed and the Egyptian dawn patrols had returned to base where the pilots were now having their breakfast, while many pilots and ground crew were still making their way to work. And then there was Field Marshal Abd el Hakim Amer. On this particular day, he decided to inspect his forces in the Sinai in company with the commander of the air force, General Mohammed Sidqi Mahmoud. Lacking total confidence in their men, all anti-aircraft batteries along their route were given strict instructions not to fire on any aircraft while the

Operation *Moked*

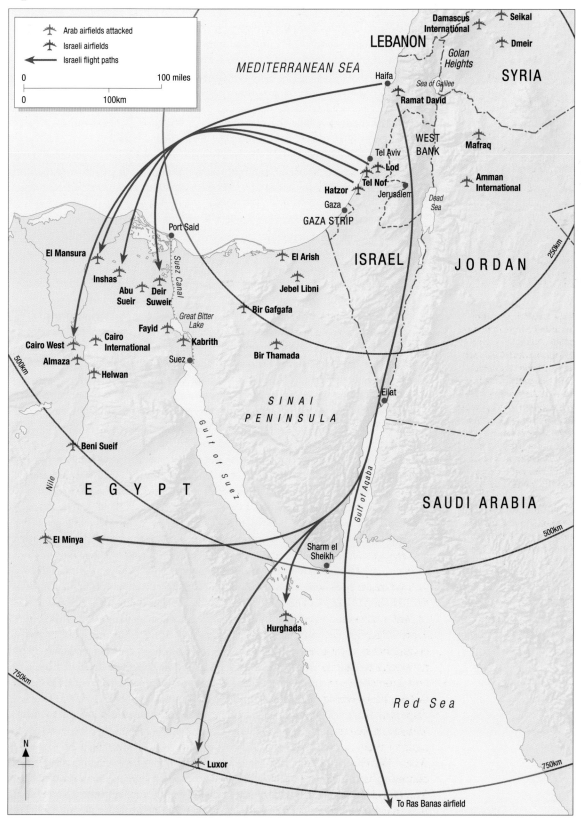

Arab airfields attacked
Israeli airfields
Israeli flight paths

0   100 miles
0   100km

MEDITERRANEAN SEA

Damascus International · Seikal

LEBANON · Dmeir

Golan Heights

SYRIA

Haifa

Sea of Galilee

Ramat David

WEST BANK

Mafraq

Tel Aviv

Lod

Tel Nof

Hatzor

Gaza

Jerusalem

Amman International

Dead Sea

GAZA STRIP

ISRAEL

JORDAN

Port Said

El Mansura

El Arish

Suez Canal

Inshas

Jebel Libni

Abu Sueir

Deir Suweir

Bir Gafgafa

Great Bitter Lake

Fayid

Kabrith

Cairo West

Cairo International

Almaza

Suez

Bir Thamada

Helwan

Eilat

S I N A I
P E N I N S U L A

Gulf of Suez

Gulf of Aqaba

Beni Sueif

E G Y P T

Nile

SAUDI ARABIA

500km

250km

El Minya

Sharm el Sheikh

500km

Hurghada

Red Sea

750km

N

Luxor

To Ras Banas airfield

750km

33

lumbering Antonov 12 transport aircraft was airborne. In the Sinai, all the senior commanders were assembled at Bir Thamada airbase to await the visit of their commander-in-chief, with some being far from their units. With the Egyptian air defence system stood down and the majority of the 82 Egyptian radar sites pointing eastwards towards Israel, the Israeli air armada thundered in from the west. Some distance short of their respective targets the four-aircraft formations climbed to an altitude of 2,750m (9,000ft) to begin their bombing runs. Visibility was excellent since the angle of the low sun delineated the targets with prominent shadows while the wind speeds at low altitude were minimal to aid accurate bombing runs. Conditions were little short of ideal.

Even so the execution of Operation *Moked* required consummate flying skills as Captain Avihu Bin-Nun, later commander of the IAF during the Gulf War of 1991, recalls as he flew his Mystère towards the Egyptian coastline:

> The flight over the sea was at especially low altitude so that the Jordanian radar could not warn the Egyptians. Our target was the Faid [Fayid] airfield, west of the Suez Canal, in the area of the Great Bitter Lake. The field was home to three combat squadrons: one of MiG-19s, one of MiG-21s and one of Sukhoi SU-7s. My formation was the first and ten minutes behind us were three more. Our secondary mission was to strike the batteries of SA-2 ground-to-air missiles on the east side of the canal. We could not miss. The formation that I led included a deputy leader, who was a reservist, and two very junior pilots who had less than a year's flying experience. The four of us took off as planned. The flight over the Mediterranean was so low that we left a wake behind us. All four of us were in place, but Number Four did not maintain a steady altitude. I was very concerned, since flying over the sea is very dangerous if one's altitude is not constant; there had been cases of inexperienced pilots flying into the ocean. I could do nothing to help and could not say a word. … Our plan of attack was to climb over the target, dive-bomb and then fire our 30-mm guns at the planes on the field. If we failed in this mission and all the other formations encountered similar conditions, the result could be fateful for the future of the State of Israel. The sky gradually cleared as we approached the target. As we came closer, the clouds dispersed enough to let us carry out the attack as planned. As I began my climb, I turned on the radio and realized that it was not working! I was not especially worried since the formation had been trained to attack in radio silence. As I dived and released my bombs, I saw four MiG-21s at the end of the runway lining up to take off. I pulled the bomb release, began firing and hit two of the four, which went up in flames. When I looked up I saw a huge Antonov 12 cargo plane landing in front of me. The Antonov's pilot saw the MiGs blowing up and turned south. I was in a dilemma – should I shoot him down, or go on with the attack as planned? Since I couldn't contact the formation and because of the importance of destroying all the MiGs on the field, I decided to carry on as planned. During the attack we destroyed 16 of the 40 MiGs scattered around the field and paralysed the SA-2 battery on our way back. During the flight home, we could see all the other Egyptian airfields in flames. I even managed to fix the problem with the radio and heard the encouraging reports.

Thus Field Marshal Amer and Gen. Sidqi Mamoud escaped death at the hands of a future commander of the IAF. It was a fortunate decision on the latter's part as Amer's subsequent abysmal conduct of the war was a significant factor in the overall Israeli victory.

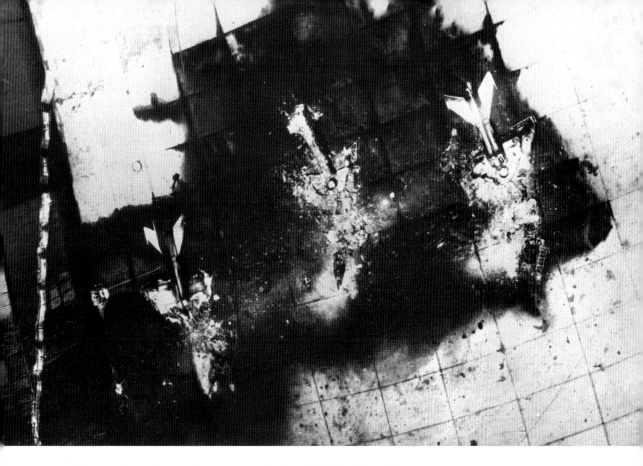

At airbase after airbase, Operation *Moked* unfolded with awful precision. Repeated four-ship formations each made their initial bombing runs with either Durandal runway-piercing or general-purpose bombs followed by three strafing runs against the unprotected Egyptian fighters and bombers – often lined up wing tip to wing tip for easier destruction. In the space of 20 minutes each airbase was struck three times. The priority targets were the Tupolev Tu-16 bombers that were capable of attacking every Israeli town and city. Second on the target list were the supersonic fighters such as the MiG-21, then subsonic fighters and finally transport planes and helicopters. All strafing runs were conducted at as low an altitude as possible to maximize hit probability, conserve ammunition and allow for the identification of decoys. The pilots were instructed to keep in reserve a third of their fuel and a third of their cannon ammunition for air-to-air combat. It was hardly necessary as few Egyptian fighters took to the skies since their runways were attacked in a very specific manner as Brigadier-General Tahsin Zaki, an Egyptian airbase commander recalled: 'I heard the noise of jet planes and I looked toward the direction of the noise and saw two grey Super Mystère planes. They dropped two bombs at the beginning of the runway. Two additional planes were behind them and they dropped their bombs in the middle of the runway and the last two planes dropped two bombs at the end of the runway. After a couple of minutes the whole runway was bombed. It was a complete surprise.' By 0800hrs (0900hrs Egyptian time), two airbases in Egypt and four in the Sinai had been completely destroyed. The first wave of attacks lasted for 80 minutes. There was then a lull for ten minutes before a second wave of attacks lasting another 80 minutes fell upon the hapless Egyptians. Within 170 minutes, the Egyptian Air Force lost 293 aircraft or almost two a minute including all

Three MiG-21 jet fighters lie burnt and shattered in the aftermath of Operation *Moked*. As the commander of the IAF, Brig. Gen. Mordechai Hod, observed 'A fighter jet is the deadliest weapon in existence – in the sky. But on the ground it is utterly defenceless.' The success of Operation *Moked*, or *Focus* in English, was the key to the Israeli victory in the Six Day War. In his Order of the Day of 7 June, the GOC Southern Command, Brig. Gen. Yeshayahu Gavish, praised the IAF by paraphrasing the words of Winston Churchill during the Battle of Britain 'Never before have so few pilots destroyed so many aircraft in such a short time.'

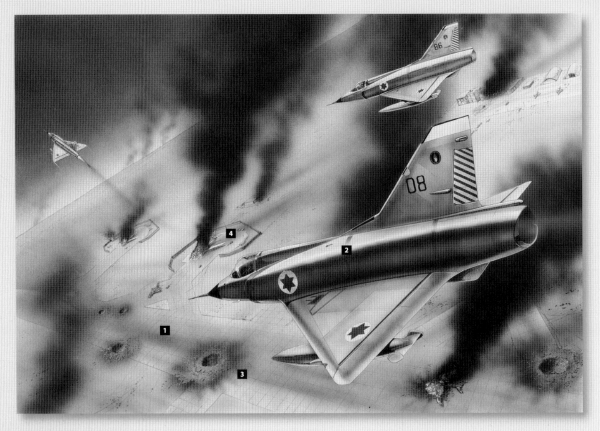

OPERATION *MOKED*, CAIRO WEST, 5 JUNE 1967 (pp. 36–37)

Israel's primary strategy at the outbreak of war was to undertake a pre-emptive strike against the opposing Arab air forces. The intention was to cripple their capability to attack population centres in Israel and cause mass civilian casualties. The plan originated in the early 1960s with the procurement of the Dassault Mirage IIICJ fighter-bomber to supplement the other ground attack aircraft of French manufacture then in service with the IAF. Codenamed Operation *Moked* in Hebrew or *Focus* in English, the plan was revised and refined over the years and provided various options in times of open hostilities: *Moked A* was an attack against Egypt only; *Moked B* against Syria only; *Moked C* against Egypt and Syria or against Egypt, Syria and Jordan; while *Moked D* was against Egypt, Iraq, Jordan, Lebanon and Syria. In the event, the IAF struck the airbases of Egypt, Iraq, Jordan and Syria on the opening day of the war. Flying in low from the Mediterranean Sea to avoid radar detection, the three- and four-aircraft formations made one bombing run to disable the runways followed by three strafing passes with 30mm cannon fire to destroy as many aircraft on the ground as possible. This scene depicts the second attack on Cairo West airbase (**1**) by Mission 101/4 during Operation *Moked*. Having taken off at 0737hrs, these *Shahak* aircraft of No. 101 Squadron (**2**)

– First Fighter Squadron – were flown by flight leader Amos Amir in Callsign Potal 1 with the others in the formation by Maoz Poraz (Potal 2), Yithak Barzilai (Potal 3) and Yochal Richter (Potal 4). The attack was undertaken at H+25 or 0810hrs (0910hrs local) with three aircraft each carrying two general-purpose 500kg bombs and Potal 1 with 70kg runway-piercing bombs and the heavier version known as *Ollar Had* or Sharp Pocketknife. Some 500kg bombs were fitted with 7-15 delay detonators to enable the weapon to penetrate the runway and then explode beneath the surface before exploding and causing a larger bomb crater. The scene shows the impact of the smaller runway-piercing bombs that penetrated and then lay dormant with delayed-action fuses set to explode at varying periods in order to discourage repairs being undertaken to the damaged runways (**3**). This formation bombed Runway 10/28 at Cairo West. Following the bombing run, Potal 1 (*Shahak* 34) is seen making a strafing pass at a Tupolev Tu-16 Badger bomber (**4**) in its protective hardstand. Cairo West was the principal Egyptian Tu-16 airbase and these strategic bombers were the priority targets as they were capable of striking any town or city in Israel. During this particular mission, two Tupolev Tu-16 bombers and a MiG-21 fighter were destroyed.

30 Tupolev Tu-16 long-range bombers; 27 Ilyushin Il-28 medium bombers; 12 Sukhoi Su-7 fighter-bombers; 90 MiG-21s; 20 MiG-19s; 75 MiG-17s and over 30 assorted transport planes and helicopters as well as trainers. The IAF losses in the first wave were ten aircraft including three Super Mystères, two Mystères, four Ouragans and one Fouga Magister with six others badly damaged. Six pilots were killed including one whose stricken aircraft strayed over Dimona and was destroyed by an Israeli Hawk missile.

Back in the Pit, the IDF High Command remained on tenterhooks as the initial reports of success were received but Brig. Gen. Hod refused to confirm them until he had personally debriefed his squadron commanders. Nevertheless Gen. Dayan issued the *Red Sheet* codeword at 0750hrs. The ground war in the Sinai could begin. After further consultation, Hod finally turned to his Chief of Staff, Maj. Gen. Rabin, at 1045hrs and said 'The Egyptian Air Force has ceased to exist.' Brigadier-General Weizman telephoned his wife with the words 'We have won the war!' At 1245hrs, the IAF was unleashed against Jordan, Syria and Iraq. Within 30 minutes, the whole Jordanian Air Force of 28 aircraft was destroyed in just 52 sorties. The Syrian Air Force lost two-thirds of its strength in one afternoon with 57 aircraft destroyed on the ground while the Iraqi airbase at H3 was also attacked with the loss of another ten aircraft. The rest fled into the hinterland. By nightfall of 6 June, the IAF had destroyed 416 Arab combat planes with 393 on the ground. In the same time, 26 Israeli aircraft were lost in action, mostly to ground fire. Operation *Moked* had succeeded beyond anyone's wildest imagination. The IAF was now free to provide close air support to the IDF ground forces as they plunged deep into the Sinai where the Egyptians lay vulnerable to the terrible combination of bombs, rockets, napalm and cannon that was now to be unleashed upon them. By the end of the war, the IAF destroyed 450 enemy aircraft at a cost of 46 aircraft and 20 aircrew, or almost 25 per cent of its front-line strength. The pilots of the *Chel Ha'Avir* had done it right. As Brig. Gen. Tahsin Zaki observed 'Israel spent years preparing for this war whereas we prepared for parades. The drills for the annual Revolution Day parade went on for weeks ... but there were no preparations for war.' Not since Pearl Harbor has an initial air strike been so devastating and Operation *Moked* remains one of the most decisive in the annals of air warfare whereby the outcome of a war was largely determined in the first few hours. Nevertheless, much hard fighting was to follow.

FIVE DAYS OF WAR

RED SHEET UNFOLDS

Reservists partake of a meal in the field as they wait for the codeword *Red Sheet* and the start of the campaign in the Sinai. In the words of a popular song of the time 'They gave us tasteless food and an Uzi gun.' Well motivated and generally well led, the IDF reservists were more than a match for their Arab adversaries for whom hatred of the 'Zionist entity' was no substitute for proper training and leadership.

The area in which the breakthrough battle was to take place was mainly a wide expanse of sand dunes, offering minimal cover from both observation and enemy fire. It was also virtually rainless so there was little vegetation – an arid wilderness in every sense of the word. The southern part of the Gaza Strip was fairly well populated but apart from the small desert town of El Arish, the population of northern Sinai was much sparser. Along the coast was a belt of sand dunes, fingers of which pushed down southwards into the Negev Desert and northern Sinai. South of this belt of sand, the region was a mixture of hills and wadis, criss-crossed by a number of roads and tracks. Anyone leaving the roads or rough dirt tracks in a vehicle or even on foot ran the risk of getting badly stuck in the deep, shifting sand dunes. Beyond this area were the southern mountains. After 1956, the Egyptians had spent a great deal of time, money and effort restoring many of the roads and fortifications that had been destroyed in the 1956 campaign and had transformed north-west Sinai into a large fortified area – a firm base from which to mount an offensive against Israel. Another road had been laid through the mountainous Giddi Pass that runs parallel to the Suez Canal, providing additional flexibility, while more north to south roads had been added and a series of large well-defended strongpoints had been built – including airfields, training camps and storage depots. All these combined to form a defensive framework that stretched back from the border deep into central Sinai. The Gaza Strip itself was now a well-defended fortress, with dug-in tanks and anti-tank guns, together with supporting artillery. This then was the area into which Egyptian forces had poured from May 1967 onwards and this was the area in which the *ugdas* of Southern Command were obliged to fight.

ADVANCE AT ALL COSTS – UGDA TAL, 5 JUNE

During the night of 4/5 June, Israeli forces under strict radio silence advanced stealthily, in order not to alert the Egyptians, towards the border where they waited. Then at 0750hrs the password *Red Sheet* arrived by landline telephone and immediately all the radios were switched on, breaking radio silence for the first time in almost three weeks. Clouds of blue smoke plumed into the early morning air as tank engines burst into life. The waiting units moved out to

The Israeli coastal attack to El Arish

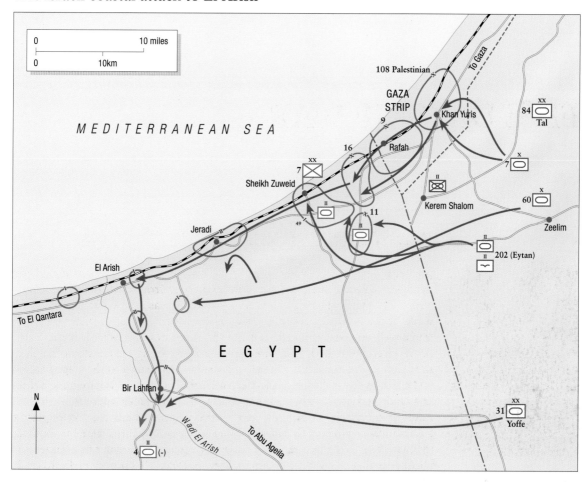

cross the border at two locations – the first opposite Nahal Oz (a kibbutz in southern Israel located in the north-west of the Negev Desert, close to the border with the Gaza Strip) and the second just to the south of Khan Yunis. They moved at best speed, holding their fire in order to prolong the element of surprise with the first elements crossing the border at about 0815hrs. Part of the 7th Brigade reconnaissance company led the way across the border at the northern crossing, moving in single file to minimize the threat from mines. Behind them were the engineers, clearing a path through the minefields and marking it with white strips and coloured flags. However, as the head of the column came to the narrow streets in the outskirts of Khan Yunis they were fired upon and soon a number of burning recce vehicles was blocking the route. It rapidly became apparent that there were considerably more enemy troops in Khan Yunis than had been expected – possibly up to brigade strength rather than the battalion that had been anticipated. Behind the reconnaissance vehicles, the spearhead of the 7th Armored Brigade's northern thrust was the 79th Tank Battalion equipped with M48A2C Patton tanks, followed by the 82nd Tank Battalion equipped with Centurion tanks, then brigade headquarters with the commander Colonel Schmuel Gonen. He quickly appraised the situation and decided to send the Patton battalion right flanking around the enemy, while half of the Centurion battalion went straight on. The rest of the Centurions initially remained in reserve under the deputy

The crew of an M51 Sherman rest beneath the camouflage net of their shrouded tank in the Negev Desert. In the days just before the war, the Israelis indulged in psychological warfare by showing newsreels of IDF soldiers lounging on the beaches of Tel Aviv and reservists idling away their time in the field in order to lull the Egyptians into a false sense of security.

brigade commander, Lieutenant-Colonel 'Pinko' Harel, an outstanding officer who had already become a living legend in the IAC. Finally, the brigade's mechanized infantry battalion was sent to occupy Kerem Shalom, near the border crossing point, in case of an enemy counterattack. As the assault by 7th Armored Brigade was being launched, the *ugda*'s reconnaissance group, under the command of Lieutenant-Colonel Yisrael Granit, moved out to establish a blocking position to the south at the edge of the desert dunes, thus sealing off the battlefield from that direction.

The attack had suffered a difficult start, especially for the leading recce elements. An officer of the unit, Captain Ori Orr, recalled, 'Artillery shells, machine guns, anti-tank guns. Everything fired at us. ... Along the whole area Egyptian T-34 tanks took their positions and fired. A shell hit an Israeli half-track before it could get off the road. All eight soldiers inside were killed.' However, Khan Yunis railway station, an obvious landmark, had been nominated as the battalion RV in their preliminary orders, so the CO was able to rally his troops there and regain control. The sudden appearance of some 60 Israeli tanks in the town had completely unnerved the Palestinian garrison and they began to surrender in droves. Unfortunately, as there were no mechanized infantry available to take them prisoner, since they had been sent to hold Kerem Shalom, the enemy soldiers soon reoccupied their battle positions. Indeed, once the initial shock had worn off they proved a formidable opponent for the following Israeli infantry, holding out for three more days of bitter fighting. That did not slow down advance of 7th Armored Brigade, who now continued towards Rafah Junction – the leading Pattons pressing forwards along the railway tracks with the Centurions on the main road and the reconnaissance company leading the way. Once again all did not go smoothly for the reconnaissance troops when the Egyptians allowed them to come within a few hundred metres of Rafah Junction before springing an

unexpected ambush and revealing that a far larger force was holding the position than had been expected. However, Col. Gonen ordered another two-pronged assault, sending his Centurions along the main road with the Pattons to the west of it. The Patton column then split into two halves, one moving along the edge of the dunes to the north, then swinging around to assault Rafah from the west, while the rest of the battalion put in a frontal attack. The Israelis were now engaging the enemy with four separate thrusts all from different directions. The Egyptian commanders were utterly confused, firstly by the unexpected direction of these attacks and also by the ferocity and speed of the Israeli assaults. While these operations were taking place, the enemy put in a counterattack from the south-west with a battalion of T-34/85 tanks. It drove straight into the middle of the Israeli pincer movement and was repulsed with heavy losses.

A Patton company commander in 79th Armored Battalion, Captain Avigdor Kahalani, recalled

> As we passed through the outskirts of Rafah village white flags were flying all over the streets. Our troops must have already passed through but not a single soul was in sight. I searched for an exit, found the railway tracks and followed these until I came to the UN camp right on top of a hill overlooking the road below. From above, the Egyptians were firing and lobbing grenades at our passing tanks. Our gunners traversed the barrels of their 90mms and elevated, only to find that the angle was too steep and we could not reach the top of the hill. I then ordered some tanks to draw back and fire HE shells up the hill slope. The Egyptians vanished swiftly. We continued and soon met up with the rest of the battalion. A quick orders group that was attended by the brigadier, sent us into battle, storming right into the Egyptian 7th Infantry Division defences at Rafah Junction.

However, these initial Israeli successes were short lived and around 1000hrs the vanguard of the Patton battalion was met with heavy fire from enemy anti-tank guns to the west of the camp. Three Pattons were hit and set on fire, while the rest were forced to take up hull-down positions and engage the enemy tanks at long range. Soon several Egyptian T-34/85s were hit and disintegrated as their ammunition exploded. Then a series of heavy artillery barrages ranged in on the Israeli tanks. The reconnaissance company was

LEFT
The British-built Centurion tank was the mainstay of the IAC during the Six Day War, by which time the majority had been rearmed with the L7 105mm gun that proved to be devastating against the Soviet-supplied tanks of the Arab armies.

RIGHT
A column of M3 half-tracks prepares to move off at the outset of the war. In IDF service all half-tracks were designated M3 irrespective of their original specification. With their usual flair for improvization, the M3 half-track was developed into several different special-purpose variants, such as mortar and anti-tank gun carriers.

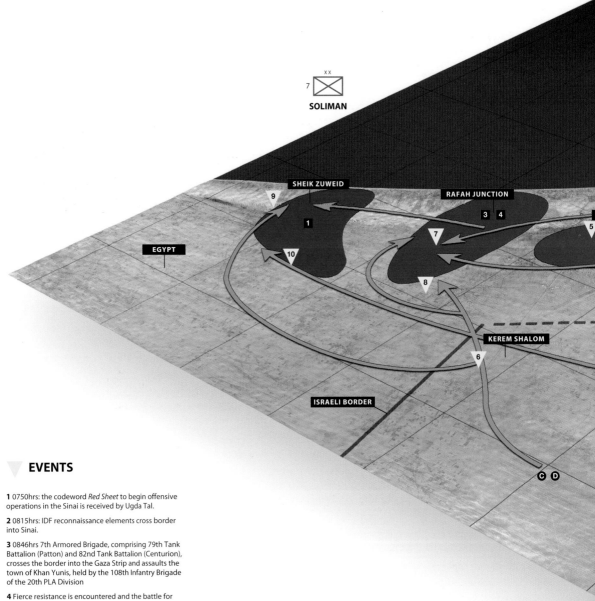

EVENTS

1 0750hrs: the codeword *Red Sheet* to begin offensive operations in the Sinai is received by Ugda Tal.

2 0815hrs: IDF reconnaissance elements cross border into Sinai.

3 0846hrs 7th Armored Brigade, comprising 79th Tank Battalion (Patton) and 82nd Tank Battalion (Centurion), crosses the border into the Gaza Strip and assaults the town of Khan Yunis, held by the 108th Infantry Brigade of the 20th PLA Division

4 Fierce resistance is encountered and the battle for Khan Yunis continues until approximately 1000hrs.

5 1020hrs: the 7th Armored Brigade splits into two for the advance on Rafah, with the 79th Tank Battalion on the northern axis and the 82nd Tank Battalion to the south.

6 Meanwhile, the 60th Armored Brigade and the 202nd Parachute Brigade, supported by the 46th Tank Battalion, separately negotiate difficult terrain to outflank the Egyptian positions from the south.

7 1200hrs: the 82nd Tank Battalion storms through the Rafah Junction stronghold while the 79th Battalion outflanks it to the north.

8 Simultaneously, the paratroopers attack Rafah Junction from the south and capture the position after hard fighting.

9 1330hrs: the 79th Tank Battalion and the 202nd Parachute Brigade capture the HQ of the Egyptian 7th Infantry Brigade at Sheik Zuweid.

10 The 60th Armored Brigade continues the advance towards the Jeradi defile and forms blocking positions against any possible counterattack. By nightfall the 7th Infantry Division is broken.

THE BATTLE OF RAFAH JUNCTION, 5 JUNE

Ugda Tal advances through the Gaza Strip and breaks through on the coastal road

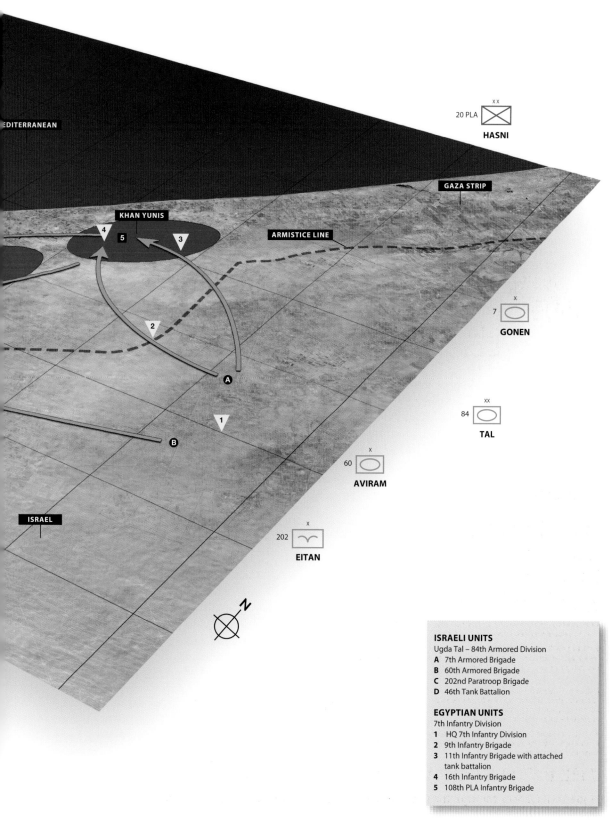

20 PLA x x
HASNI

MEDITERRANEAN

GAZA STRIP

KHAN YUNIS

4 5 3

ARMISTICE LINE

7 x
GONEN

2

84 xx
TAL

A

1

B

60 x
AVIRAM

ISRAEL

202 x
EITAN

N

ISRAELI UNITS
Ugda Tal – 84th Armored Division
A   7th Armored Brigade
B   60th Armored Brigade
C   202nd Paratroop Brigade
D   46th Tank Battalion

EGYPTIAN UNITS
7th Infantry Division
1   HQ 7th Infantry Division
2   9th Infantry Brigade
3   11th Infantry Brigade with attached
      tank battalion
4   16th Infantry Brigade
5   108th PLA Infantry Brigade

The view from the troop compartment of an M3 half-track as the vehicles of the 202nd Paratroop Brigade advance towards Rafah Junction on the opening day of the war. The plethora of radio antennae on the leading half-track indicates that it is a command vehicle.

called forward to identify potential targets but the Pattons' attack had clearly stalled. Lieutenant-Colonel 'Pinko' Harel quickly realized that he must get the attack moving again. He led his two reserve Centurion companies around to the south in a daring outflanking movement that smashed through the enemy lines, with the Centurions firing their main armament while on the move. The enemy were shocked by this audacious attack and hardly reacted at all as Harel's force pressed forwards on their way westwards. Dubbing it his 'Devil's Ride', Harel later recalled:

My orders were to take the two Centurion 105mm companies of 82nd Tank Battalion and to strike west towards Rafah Camp. Racing around the outer minefield, I made straight for the camp and started to engage enemy tanks at long range. The Egyptians were now under full alert and covered my approach with heavy artillery and mortar fire. Overhead I saw some Fouga trainers, turned into makeshift fighter bombers, swooping into the fray, firing rockets onto the enemy positions ahead. Moving slowly south, to outflank the outer enemy positions, I received orders to go at top speed to Rafah Junction where Ori's recce company was in trouble. This was what I was waiting for! Ordering my tanks into line, we charged straight ahead into the enemy position, crashing through their lines with main guns and machine guns blazing! To our right were some friendly Pattons engaged in a sharp battle with dug-in T-34s. After our crazy race through enemy fire we reached the high ground and took stock. All my tanks seemed intact, although two or three were smoking badly. Many had lost their bazooka plates. Behind us and below, dozens of enemy tanks were flaming hulks, their crews running frantically in shock and horror. But now I saw my chance to do some real tank fighting. To my right there seemed to be the objective as given to 7th Armored Brigade. Rallying my two companies and after a quick orders group, we set off at top speed before the enemy could recover their senses and realise what we were up to. But not for long! As my spearhead, led by Capt. Aaron, climbed up the desert track leading to the road, the entire front exploded into fire. Tanks, anti-tank guns and mortars were firing. The first three Centurions got through safely, but the fourth exploded in flames. I shouted to continue the race and my tanks followed me through the curtain of fire – and we made it! Once on the main road I ordered my driver to speed up and, looking back, I was delighted to see 17 Centurions all following me in column. We had crashed through two enemy outposts guarding the highway. Their soldiers were so surprised they didn't even open fire. Then we reached the rail crossing at Jeradi, perhaps the most heavily defended position east of El Arish. So far we had passed through the heavy defences without firing, but Jeradi was different. There was no hope to crash through their heavy defences without firing. I ordered my tanks to traverse right and left, and to increase speed, whilst firing with all weapons, loading with HE to create maximum shock effect. And it worked! The Egyptians were apparently taken by surprise, nor had they been warned of our approach by their outposts and didn't even fire back at us. Then, suddenly we were through and on our way to El Arish, now less than 20km away. I looked at my watch – it showed 1545hrs. After half an hour or so, I radioed brigade and told them I was within gun range of the El Arish outskirts. I was myself totally amazed at what we had achieved so far. With incredible luck we had been able to storm through no less than four heavily defended localities, losing just one tank in the process, so far so good. However, what worried me most now was being miles away from the brigade, low on fuel and ammunition, what should we do now until the main body arrived? We did not realise that Jeradi would close down tight, when the Egyptian commander

The M48A2C Patton tanks of the 79th Tank Battalion, 7th Armored Brigade, deploy into battle formation during the assault on Rafah Junction on 5 June 1967. During the Six Day War, the majority of the Israeli Pattons were still armed with the original 90mm gun.

recovered from his shock. It would take three savage battles with heavy losses to finally open the way to us. Luckily we held out, well hidden, surviving only a few minor attacks by the enemy who were hardly aware of our presence so deep in their rear!

Earlier that day, when Harel and his force had been on their way to the enemy rear, the Patton battalion had been in a serious firefight with the Egyptian main position while the remaining Centurions had reached Rafah camp and were about to join up with the Pattons. Avigdor Kahalani recalled 'From above the escarpment, the desert battlefield seemed enormous. I decided to spread my company in line for a charge and with the rest of 79th Tank Battalion under the command of Lt. Col. Ehud Elad, we stormed into the fray, with guns blazing in the best of tankers tradition!' An overexcited company commander now describes the scene:

No sooner had we passed the outer defences, the first Egyptian T-34/85 long-barrelled gun fired at me, the round missing me by inches. The tank following me quickly sighted on the enemy tank, half hidden in its sand berm and destroyed it with a 90mm AP round. But then the entire front exploded in noisy pandemonium. All at once dozens of dug-in tanks, anti-tank guns of all shapes and sizes, mortars and artillery exploded into action, filling the sky with an overwhelming, suffocating, acrid stench entering our nostrils. It was terrifying for the young tank crews who had never been in action before. Here and there tanks were blazing, some of them enemy, others ours, tankers on both sides scrambling out of their blazing hulks, trying to escape the fire, shrapnel and bullets. Many were completely dazed by the noise and fear, but the charge went on, deep into the enemy positions until the main body reached the Junction.

TOP
A Sikorsky S-58 helicopter of No. 124 'Rolling Sword' Squadron evacuates wounded soldiers after the battle of Rafah Junction. The primary role of the 'Rolling Sword' squadron was search and rescue of downed pilots during Operation *Moked*. Thereafter, they were employed for other roles such as casualty evacuation and the insertion of paratroopers.

BOTTOM
An Israeli soldier returns fire at a sniper's position in the main street of Gaza. After the initial stiff resistance of its 59th Brigade at Khan Yunis and at the Ali Muntar Ridge, the 20th Division of the Palestine Liberation Army rapidly collapsed as a coherent force although fierce fighting continued against isolated pockets throughout the Gaza Strip.

Israeli troops leave the PLO offices in Gaza after searching the building. On the gate pillars are posters bearing the image of Ahmad al-Shuqayri, the leader of the PLO, whose rhetoric espousing the destruction of Israel was excessive even by the standards of the Arab street. However, he spent the war safely ensconced in Damascus.

Meanwhile, further south, Col. Raful Eitan's 202nd Paratroop Brigade had started its attack and had made contact with the main Egyptian positions that it had begun to mop up with the paratroops clearing the enemy trenches in bitter hand-to-hand fighting. This task was not made any easier because of a lack of basic tank/infantry cooperation training – not a normal task for paratroopers. This was apparent when most of the tanks fanned out and drove off, leaving the vulnerable paratroopers with only a handful of tanks to support them. This soon became critical because, for once the Egyptians reacted quickly, and, being now on full alert, they moved up some heavy IS-3M tanks of the Egyptian 7th Infantry Division. The first major tank vs. tank battle of the war began in earnest. The IS-3M, with its distinctive-shaped front glacis plate earning it the nickname of the 'Pike', mounted a formidable 122mm main armament as compared with the Patton's standard 90mm. Fortunately, in this case these Pattons were some of the few that had been up-gunned with the L7 105mm gun. As the Stalins appeared over the sand ridges, a company of Pattons from Lieutenant-Colonel Uri Bar-On's 46th Tank Battalion that had been on their way to assist Lt. Col. Yisrael Granit's reconnaissance group, stormed forwards and began engaging them. One of the Patton commanders, Captain Shalom Ein Gil, recalled this encounter:

Having heard the order to turn north, I followed Capt. Amnon Giladi's tank when it suddenly exploded in a ball of fire. I could see Amnon slumped over the commander's cupola, seemingly already dead. I immediately took evasive action, outflanking the blazing tank and traversing to search for the source of the enemy fire. In my hurry I turned too far and found myself heading directly for the enemy anti-tank guns, which all fired directly at me. At full speed I shot through the position, guns blazing, squashing men and guns as we went, followed by the rest of the company. Amazingly, after losing our company commander, we all survived the terrifying charge. I was now leading the company with nine tanks following me. As we crossed a sand dune I saw two enemy tanks, about 2,000 metres away, but could not identify them at first, believing them naturally to be T-34s. However, as we got closer it dawned on me that they were much larger vehicles – in fact they turned out to be the Stalin Monsters, the dreaded menace that Uri had warned us about during his orders group! No sooner had I recognised my opponents then I expected them to immediately open fire with their big guns. There were six of them now, all in line, but strangely not moving or even traversing their monstrous turrets at us. All our gunners were quickly on target. Without me having to give any orders, they fired their 105mm guns, loaded with APDS. All scored hits. The enemy crews attention must have been distracted to the north for some reason. Totally surprised by our appearance out of nowhere, two Stalins were soon on fire and blazing. Now the rest of their crews tried frantically to change position and to fire at us. But they were too slow – they fired, but we had moved, so they missed. Having taken up hull-down positions Sgt. Benny Inbar and my own gunner set another three Stalins on fire, hitting them in their vulnerable rear and sides. Within minutes ten Stalins were blazing in the sand, their surviving crews stumbling frantically out of the blazing steel hulks. A few had been hit so hard, that their heavy turrets virtually flew off. It was a terrifying scene of carnage. Once we met up with Col. Granit's force we were told that the very Stalins that we had just destroyed had actually been fighting his small force, causing deadly casualties. He must have been delighted with our appearance just at the right moment.

In addition, some IAF Fouga Magister trainers that had been converted into the ground attack role suddenly appeared on the scene and began low-level rocket attacks on the remaining enemy tanks while the Pattons, exploiting their success, broke through, making contact with the main enemy anti-tank complex to the rear. There they knocked out several tanks and anti-tank guns, all static in bunker positions. With the enemy tank threat now considerably reduced, the paratroopers went on to clear the rest of the trenches. Help had also come from Brig. Gen. Tal who, realizing that the paratroopers were in difficulty, ordered Col. Gonen to send his Pattons to support them. He also diverted the mechanized infantry battalion that had been left holding Kerem Shalom and sent them forwards as well.

By noon, two separate battles were being fought around Rafah Junction: one in the south, by the paratroop brigade which, after fighting through the southern Egyptian positions with their supporting Pattons, pressed on to

A classic portrait of an IDF tank commander epitomizes the proficiency and determination of Israel's citizen-soldiers. In just six days, the IDF destroyed the armies of three Arab nations in an awesome display of blitzkrieg or lightning war. It is one of history's rich ironies that arguably the most complete example of blitzkrieg ever was undertaken by the Jews in a campaign that altered the whole strategic balance in the Middle East to this day.

the rear of the enemy main anti-tank complex. The Egyptian divisional headquarters that was located nearby was also overrun, the GOC killed and his headquarters demolished. Meanwhile, Lt. Col. Harel's Centurions had pushed on towards Jeradi, while in the north another fierce battle was in progress with the remainder of the 7th Armored Brigade fighting their way into the northern area of the Egyptian defences. Later that afternoon, a multi-pronged attack was mounted with the paratroop brigade and its remaining tanks, attacking to the north in a bid to link up with 7th Armored Brigade, which was now attacking to the south. During this action, the brigade's mechanized infantry battalion was called in, reaching the Junction just as the *ugda*'s tactical command group arrived to control this critical situation at close quarters.

The battle reached its climax at around 1500hrs with a determined effort to subdue the last enemy resistance. Just then word was received from 'Pinko' Harel that he had reached the outskirts of El Arish and had established a blocking position there, but was short of both fuel and ammunition. His two Centurion companies had broken through the entire enemy position along the 20km stretch of road, smashing their way through two enemy brigade positions with hardly any losses. It was now up to the *ugda* to link up with Harel's isolated force before the enemy brought up superior numbers against them. With the battle for Rafah Junction virtually over, Brig. Gen. Tal now planned his next move. The 60th Armored Brigade would outflank and then attack the Jeradi complex, while the 7th Armored Brigade pushed along the main road in order to link up with Harel in a daring night move. But that was only the beginning, now the Jeradi position was waiting to be stormed.

THE JERADI DEFILE – UGDA TAL, 5 JUNE

Around 1300hrs, Gonen's two tank battalions rallied at Sheikh Zuweid village for a short debrief and more orders from their brigade commander. Both Brig. Gen. Tal and Col. Gonen were determined to maintain the momentum of the advance, so the latter willingly committed one of his last two tank companies that he had been holding in reserve, together with the battered brigade reconnaissance company and ordered them to move westwards at best speed to help Harel's force at El Arish. On approaching the Jeradi defile, where the road twisted and turned down a steep sand dune into a wadi, they found the Egyptian garrison, comprising a complete battalion group, fast asleep. The tanks drove through with all guns blazing and did not suffer any casualties. However, the reconnaissance company lost some more vehicles and was forced to take up a defensive position on the near bank of the wadi. Meanwhile, the Centurions had pushed on and did not stop until they reached the deserted United Nations camp on the outskirts of El Arish. Here, however, the enemy had recovered sufficiently and prevented any immediate further advance. The Centurions were now facing the rest of the Egyptian reserve brigade. 'Clearing the city was hard fighting' states the IDF official war record, 'the Egyptians fired from the rooftops, from balconies and windows. They dropped grenades into our half-tracks and blocked the streets with trucks. Our men threw the grenades back and crushed the trucks with their tanks.'

At the Jeradi defile, Col. Gonen found that they were faced by a well-prepared enemy position on the far bank of the wadi. The wadi itself was mined and covered by enemy tanks, anti-tank guns and machine guns. There was a grove of palm trees to the north that might have provided a covered approach,

The crew of an up-gunned Centurion Mark 5 disembark from their tank during an exercise by the elite 7th Armored Brigade just prior to the Six Day War. In Israeli service the Centurion was known as *Sho't* meaning whip or scourge in Hebrew.

but it was too thick to permit tank movement while the ground to the south was open with soft sand dunes that made an assault very difficult from that flank. The Patton battalion arrived at the wadi at about 1700hrs and Col. Gonen ordered them to mount an immediate frontal assault down the road together with a flank attack over the open sand dunes to the south. Both proved unsuccessful with the frontal attack being repulsed while the flank attack bogged down in the soft sand. Lieutenant-Colonel Ehud Elad, the commander of the battalion, was killed and all three of his company commanders wounded. Out of sight of the enemy, the second in command rallied the battalion and prepared to make a further attempt at 1800hrs. He called for both air and artillery support. All the tanks closed down and rushed the enemy position, losing only one tank in the mêlée that followed. Despite breaking through the enemy position, however, it was still not a complete victory, as the Egyptians rallied and then managed to prevent the brigade command post, the remainder of the reconnaissance company, together with the brigade supply trucks that were all trying to follow up, from getting past. The new commander of the victorious Patton battalion then offered to try and clear the enemy position from the rear, in order to open the route. However, Col. Gonen instead ordered him to press on to El Arish – the *ugda*'s battle cry still being 'Advance at all costs!'

Despite the fact that they had thus managed partly to bypass the Jeradi position, it had not been captured and was still preventing Brig. Gen. Tal from achieving a cohesive link-up of his *ugda* – the Pattons and Centurions having pushed through while the infantry, artillery and supply columns were still north of the Egyptian position. Additionally, the *ugda*'s reserve, the 60th Armored Brigade of AMX-13s and Shermans was now stuck in the sand dunes having made an unsuccessful attempt to bypass the main blockage. It was now getting dark and the overall situation was not good with the *ugda* spread over some 50km (30 miles) with one and a half tank battalions of the

7th Armored Brigade at El Arish facing an entire Egyptian brigade; Col. Gonen himself and the remainder of the *ugda*'s reconnaissance company were still on the east side of the Jeradi wadi; his two remaining tank companies were in divisional reserve; the mechanized battalion group was still clearing the area to the north of Rafah; Col. Eitan's brigade was clearing the area to the south of Rafah Junction while Col. Menachem Aviram's brigade of AMX-13s/Shermans was stuck in the sand dunes to the south. Accordingly Ugda Tal had little time to dwell on their extraordinary successes to date, especially because the Egyptian 4th Armoured Division with several hundred T-54 and T-55 tanks was even now moving towards El Arish along the central Sinai road. All that Tal had in reserve was just two tank companies. Realizing this was a critical moment, Brig. Gen. Tal decided to take even greater risks and Rafah and Jeradi were to be where these risks would be taken. Colonel Gonen's mechanized infantry battalion and a Patton company were even now clearing an area at Rafah in order to secure it for the *ugda*'s supply train, but this task had become secondary to maintaining pressure on the enemy. Tal immediately released the battalion group back to Col. Gonen and added one of his two remaining tank companies. The mission he gave to this force was to clear the Jeradi defile.

Giving the order was one thing, achieving it another. But fortunately yet another remarkable man was waiting in the wings. Faced with the problem of rallying his mechanized battalion group, which was then spread over some seven kilometres (four miles), in the pitch dark, was just another problem to be faced for Lieutenant-Colonel Mordecai Avigat, the battalion commander known as being a quiet and unassuming but resourceful and enterprising officer. Getting on the radio to his company commanders, he ordered them to get their troops to return to their half-tracks and then to drive to the main road. He then motored along the road, picking up each company in turn and then led the complete unit to Brig. Gen. Tal at Rafah Junction. It is said that the delighted general kissed the CO on both cheeks. The entire *ugda* artillery was also put at his disposal, including all the night illumination rounds. The tank company was then sent on ahead to join Col. Gonen at the Jeradi defile. He deployed it so that the Egyptians could not move reinforcements from one side of the road to the other. With the Patton company at its head, Avigat then led his battalion through the press of stationary vehicles that were jamming the road to the west of Rafah Junction. No one wanted to move off the road because they feared striking a mine. However, they were physically forced out of the way so that his column could get past. On reaching the Jeradi defile, the vehicles closed up and the CO called for artillery and tank covering fire, plus an illumination shoot to light up the route. He then led his group at top speed down the road through the enemy position, to a prearranged RV at Jeradi Station – a small shack at the end of the defile and the only recognizable landmark in the dark. There he halted and placed the Pattons plus one mechanized company as a roadblock facing to the west. His two remaining companies were then formed up on either side of the road facing east and fought their way back to clear the position. It took some four hours to secure the trenches back to the beginning of the blockage on just 180m (200 yards) of frontage. At first light they continued mopping up away from the road. The battalion was then left to secure the defile whilst the remainder of the brigade passed through. Whilst this operation was taking place, the deputy brigade commander, 'Pinko' Harel, whose small force had broken through to El Arish the day before, used his one and a half armoured battalions, to

block all routes out of El Arish in order to prevent any of the Egyptian garrison from getting out and joining the action. However, he was now perilously short of ammunition and fuel. Fortunately Col. Gonen did not hesitate any longer and decided to move his supply trains through the gap. Leading the convoy himself, he gathered his trucks together, then raced through the 13km (eight-mile) Jeradi defile and managed to reach Harel's force at about 0200hrs. Replenishment began at once. By dawn it was all over. The infantry had mopped up the last enemy positions, the road to El Arish was open and large supply columns, artillery and command groups were now driving westwards at high speed. The defile at Jeradi was cleared, the remnants of its Egyptian garrison shell-shocked and defeated. In the space of 24 hours, Ugda Tal had eliminated the 7th Infantry Division and was at the outskirts of El Arish, the administrative centre of the Egyptian Army in the Sinai. In the words of Lt. Yossi Peled, a young armour officer, 'Egyptian tanks were burning for as far as we could see and Egyptian soldiers were lying between them. But many of our tanks were also ablaze and the Israelis lying beside them were no longer alive.' Israeli losses within Ugda Tal so far were 66 killed, 93 wounded and 28 tanks destroyed but the advance continued at all costs.

THE BATTLE OF BIR LAHFAN – UGDA YOFFE, 5 JUNE

Topographically Bir Lahfan presented a strategic bottleneck, a virtual 'door' into central Sinai that would become the turning point of the war in Sinai. The Egyptians had devised their defensive concept upon the assumption that their two strong, forward-deployed divisions would hold out against the Israeli attacks, which they believed would be a two-pronged offensive at Rafah and Um Katef. This would give them enough time to send their strong armoured reserves towards Bir Lahfan to block Ugda Tal along the coastal road. But the Israelis had played their trump card by sending Brig. Gen. Avraham Yoffe's *ugda* through the uncharted desert to arrive, totally unexpectedly, at Bir Lahfan, approaching from its undefended flank. As Gonen's 7th Armored Brigade had already broken through and would soon be on its way, the

LEFT
Egyptian prisoners of war are processed after the battle for El Arish. As Brig. Gen. Sharon observed in his blunt manner 'I think the Egyptian soldiers are very good. They are simple and ignorant but are strong and disciplined. They are good gunners, good diggers and good shooters but their officers are shit, they can fight only according to what they planned before.'

RIGHT
AMX-13 light tanks attached to the 11th Mechanized Brigade advance cautiously into the Gaza Strip. These tanks proved their worth during the heavy fighting for the Ali Muntar ridge that was captured after bitter hand-to-hand combat. Once this high ground overlooking Gaza City was taken, all resistance crumbled and the Gaza Strip was subdued by the morning of 7 June.

TOP

A platoon of Centurion tanks advances over typical terrain in the north-east region of the Negev and Sinai deserts, showing the major problem of operating armour in such conditions. The clouds of dust were constantly ingested into air filters. These had to be very regularly cleaned to ensure efficient operation of the tank engines.

BOTTOM

Following the Suez Campaign of 1956, the Medical Corps of the IDF made intensive trials of the optimum level of water intake for combat effectiveness in the harsh desert conditions prevailing in the region. This was found to be one pint per soldier per hour and this had to be adhered to for fear of punishment. Accordingly, the provision of water was a high priority in the IDF. In the Egyptian Army, there was a woeful lack of water among front-line troops leading to impaired efficiency and many cases of heat exhaustion.

Egyptian armoured reserves were about to enter a deadly trap. The battle of Bir Lahfan was about to unfold and would soon become one of the decisive actions of the war.

During the night Egyptian tanks had been streaming along the central Sinai roads, heading for El Arish. Before midnight they had reached Jebel Libni and were continuing northwards. However, what the enemy did not know, was that the 200th Armored Brigade, part of Ugda Yoffe, had undertaken an extraordinary advance through the supposedly impassable sand dunes of Wadi Haridin, had already reached the strategic crossroads of Bir Lahfan, on the road between El Arish and Jebel Libni, ahead of the Egyptians. One of the reservist tank commanders in the 200th Tank Brigade recalls the situation:

> Our battalion, commanded by Lt. Col. Abraham Bar-Am, a regular officer, led
> the way over an uncharted desert dune track crossing Wadi Haridin. We drove

all day long, in low gear, trying not to become bogged down in the soft desert dunes. In front of me, hardly visible from the dust, was the troop led by young Lt. Ilan Yakuel. After a short fight with an Egyptian desert post, we refuelled and by nightfall had reached the hills overlooking the macadam road leading from El Arish to Jebel Libni. In front of us I identified a radar post, its antennae still moving. The crew took no notice of our arrival and did not react at all. The colonel ordered us into attack formation and we stormed in, guns blazing at the radar station, which exploded in a fireball. Night fell as we took up blocking positions southwards, expecting any moment the arrival of enemy reinforcements from Jebel Libni, where we knew, from intelligence briefings the enemy had its armoured reserves positioned and on high alert. By now it was already totally dark and still strangely silent. Suddenly, as if to open the prelude to battle, an artillery barrage smashed onto us in a deafening crescendo. Although I was a reservist, it was my first experience of real fire and it scared the wits out of me and my crew! The bombardment continued, but surprisingly, the heavy shelling did not cause any casualties and apart from some minor damage to some of our Centurions, we all remained intact. I was dead tired, after having had no sleep during our long desert ride and the preparations before it, so I must have dozed off, when the colonel called us wide awake, announcing the arrival of enemy tanks. Two Egyptian brigades were moving in our direction! Soon I could see a long column of lights, like a string of pearls winding along in the darkness, coming right towards us some five kilometres away. We were in line with Lt. Yakuel's tank as he opened fire having been given permission from the colonel. I ordered my gunner to fire also. With our first shot, as if by magic, the entire enemy column turned off their headlights and disappeared from view! By now the enemy had advanced to about 2000 metres range, but remained invisible. I couldn't find any targets to shoot at, but then tanks around me were being hit by enemy tank fire and I realised that the enemy tanks were the dreaded T-55s with infrared (IR) night vision,

Much of the equipment employed by the IDF was procured from the French during the mid-1950s, such as the AMX-13 reconnaissance tank. Owing to a lack of battle tanks, the AMX-13 was employed for offensive operations as against its intended role purely for reconnaissance.

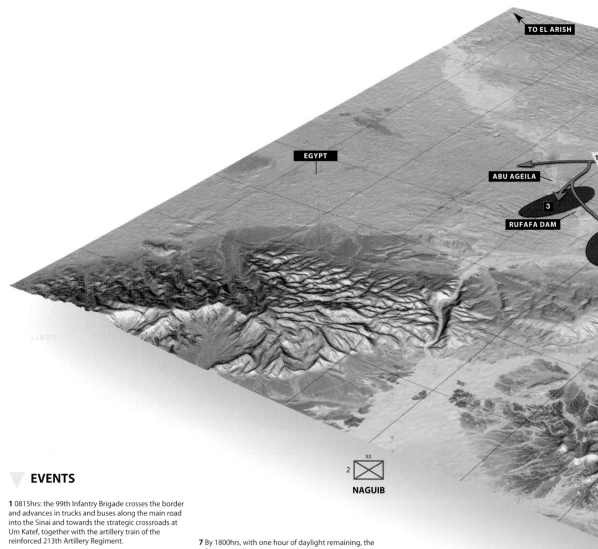

TO EL ARISH

EGYPT

ABU AGEILA

10

3

RUFAFA DAM

2 XX

NAGUIB

▼ EVENTS

1 0815hrs: the 99th Infantry Brigade crosses the border and advances in trucks and buses along the main road into the Sinai and towards the strategic crossroads at Um Katef, together with the artillery train of the reinforced 213th Artillery Regiment.

2 To the south, the tanks of the 14th Armored Brigade advance along the minor Turkish Road, although elements of the brigade are in support of the above.

3 The 226th Tank Battalion makes an outflanking movement to the north to interdict Egyptian reserves and attack infantry stronghold at Abu Ageila.

4 A Reconnaissance Task Force comprising one company of AMX-13 tanks, a company of infantry crammed into jeeps, a battery of self-propelled 120mm mortars and a platoon of combat engineers traverses difficult mountainous terrain to block any reinforcements from the south along the Abu Ageila to Quseima road.

5 Heavy resistance is encountered at Tarat Um, Um Tarpe and Hill 181 that delays the advance into the afternoon.

6 Elements of the 14th Armored Brigade engage and destroy Egyptian armour during late afternoon.

7 By 1800hrs, with one hour of daylight remaining, the infantry are advancing across the dunes under artillery fire before resting prior to the night attack while the artillery move forward within range of the whole position at Um Katef.

8 2245hrs: the largest artillery bombardment in IDF history is unleashed for 20 minutes prior to the infantry assault with one battalion attacking each of the three defence lines supported by the Sherman tanks of the 14th Armored Brigade.

9 Simultaneously, paratroopers of the 80th Paratroop Brigade land by helicopter behind enemy lines and attacks the Egyptian artillery park disabling the guns.

10 0100hrs: the Centurions of the 226th Tank Battalion attack the Egyptian armoured reserves at Abu Ageila and envelop the defences of Um Katef from the rear as well as forming a blocking position astride the road to El Arish. The battle lasted through the night but by daybreak the strongest fortification in the Sinai had fallen at a cost to the IDF of 41 dead and 140 wounded.

BATTLE OF ABU AGEILA/UM KATEF, 5/6 JUNE

Ugda Sharon assaults Egyptian fortified positions in the Sinai

Note: Gridlines are shown at intervals of 5km/3.10miles

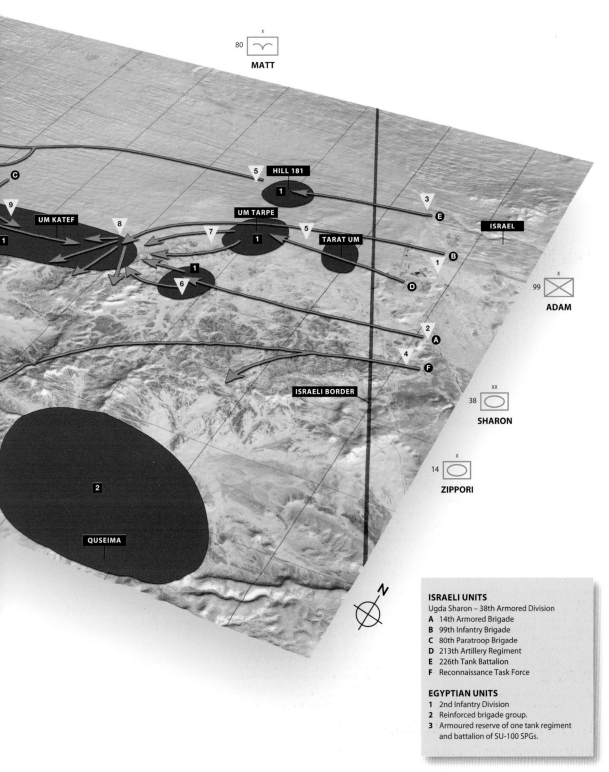

80 MATT

5 HILL 181
1

C

9

UM KATEF

1

8

7 UM TARPE
1

5

TARAT UM

3

E

ISRAEL

1 B

99 ADAM

1

6

D

2

A

4

F

ISRAELI BORDER

38 SHARON

14 ZIPPORI

2

QUSEIMA

N

ISRAELI UNITS
Ugda Sharon – 38th Armored Division
A 14th Armored Brigade
B 99th Infantry Brigade
C 80th Paratroop Brigade
D 213th Artillery Regiment
E 226th Tank Battalion
F Reconnaissance Task Force

EGYPTIAN UNITS
1 2nd Infantry Division
2 Reinforced brigade group.
3 Armoured reserve of one tank regiment and battalion of SU-100 SPGs.

59

At the forefront of the offensive in the Sinai were the reconnaissance units equipped with light vehicles for greater mobility such as these M38A1C jeeps. Accordingly they suffered significant casualties in the initial encounters with the entrenched Egyptians. Once in the open desert, these units provided invaluable intelligence to aid the overall offensive.

which we had been briefed about. We did not have any IR on our tanks, just a few had searchlight projectors. Indeed Lt. Yakuel turned his on and fired, setting three enemy tanks on fire in seconds, before his tank was hit and on fire. By now we were ordered to fire on the enemy tanks silhouetted by the blazing trucks and tanks. I then noticed that some of the Egyptian tankers were trying to outflank us through the desert, so I traversed onto them, following their progress and firing as they came into my sights. We were now firing both to the front and flanks – it was a terrifying scenario, deafening noise and the horrible stench of cordite in our nostrils. The battle went on all through the night. At first light we could see the entire battlefield covered in flaming tanks and trucks. More and more enemy tanks came forward. We were now low on ammunition, indeed, several of our tanks were already out of action as they had run out. Then, with almost perfect timing, out of nowhere swooped a flight of our Super Mystère fighter-bombers, which began strafing the enemy tanks. Then I heard a new voice on the radio. It was the 7th Armored Brigade spearhead, coming to our rescue out of El Arish! Soon their tanks came into view and raced at full speed to chase the enemy, who were now in full retreat. By 1000hrs the battle of Bir Lahfan was won and the battle at Jebel Libni was about to begin!

The following morning, the 7th and 200th armored brigades continued to push southwards and to fight their way through to the remaining Egyptian defences at Bir Lahfan. Together, the two armoured brigades from Ugdas Tal and Yoffe then defeated a final counterattack by the remaining elements of the Egyptian armoured force. The breakthrough phase was over and the Israelis had won a considerable victory. Brigadier-General Tal and his troops had achieved their mission by a mixture of daring and sheer bloody-minded perseverance. Despite the fact that the Egyptian defences had proved to be far stronger than anticipated; that the soft sand dunes had proved to be a major tank obstacle especially on the southern flank; that one brigade had shown itself to be deficient in tank/infantry cooperation and that twice the enemy had succeeded in cutting the main axis at the Jeradi defile, Tal and his men had continued to show single-minded determination not to allow any of these drawbacks to prevent them achieving their mission. Tal had taken risks and his troops had made numerous mistakes, but as an example of a successful and determined pursuit, the conduct of this part of the Sinai campaign and the overall performance of 7th Armored Brigade can have few equals. After achieving the breakthrough and capturing El Arish, Ugda Tal continued westwards and would take part in battles at Bir Gifgafa, Romani and El Qantara, on its way to the Suez Canal.

THE BATTLE FOR ABU AGEILA–UM KATEF – UGDA SHARON, 5 JUNE

The Egyptian fortification system at Abu Ageila–Um Katef had been deliberately designed by the Egyptians to block the central axis in the Sinai, namely the Nitzana–Ismailia 'gateway', which was a narrow strip of land that offered good going for vehicles of all types, both tracked and wheeled. It was bounded to the north by a belt of soft sand dunes while to the south lay the jagged ridges and broken foothills of the Jebel Dalafa. In the 1948 war, it had been easily overrun by the Israelis but in 1956 it had not been taken, instead the Egyptians had held it until they had finally abandoned it in their general withdrawal. Clearly capturing the Abu Ageila crossroads was vital, because even if Israeli armour was able to manoeuvre through much of the desert areas of Sinai, control of the main central road across the peninsula was essential for the advance of the Israeli infantry as they might well have to be moved in ordinary civilian buses rather than military trucks. It was also vital for the movement of any major logistical support units that were so important to the attacking forces.

Having learnt some salutary lessons from the past two wars, the Egyptians, with the help and advice of their Russian combat engineer advisers, had sealed this 'gateway' with a well-entrenched and heavily fortified defensive system, that, from its furthest outposts, extended to a depth of some 35km (22 miles), the strongpoints being linked together by masses and masses of barbed wire entanglements and newly sown minefields. The thickest part of this defensive system stretched from Um Katef westwards to Abu Ageila. It also guarded the road north to El Arish and the one south to Quseima, where there was another strongpoint, manned by an infantry brigade with an additional entrenched infantry battalion also guarded by minefields, together with some 90 dug-in T-34 and T-54 tanks and an equivalent number of artillery pieces, many self-propelled. Um Katef was additionally a strong natural defensive position with a ridge of hills to the south and a number of deep sand dunes to the north. These

THE BATTLE OF UM KATEF, 5/6 JUNE 1967 (pp. 62–63)

The Egyptian defences at Um Katef protecting the strategic crossroads at Abu Ageila were among the strongest in the Sinai Peninsula. Constructed in the prescribed Soviet tactical manner, the three parallel fortified lines were some five kilometres (three miles) wide made up of mutually supporting trench lines, anti-tank guns and machine-gun positions all protected by minefields up to 300m (1,000ft) deep. The massive stronghold was supported by 80 artillery pieces, 90 tanks and self-propelled guns together with 16,000 men of the 2nd Infantry Division. Although at full strength, the division was commanded by a political appointee, Maj. Gen. Sadi Naguib, who was a drinking companion of Field Marshal Abd el Hakim Amer. Opposing him was the 38th Armored Division of Brig. Gen. Ariel Sharon, one of the most experienced commanders in the IDF. Convinced that the Egyptians were far less effective fighters in the dark, Sharon devised a complex, combined-arms, night assault. At 2200hrs, the heaviest artillery barrage in the annals of the IDF was unleashed against the fortifications of Abu Ageila and Um Katef, with 6,000 shells fired in just 20 minutes. This was to be followed by infantry and armour attacks; the latter both frontally and from the flank that made coordination extremely complex and

the danger of friendly forces firing on each other increasingly likely. However, it was vital to eliminate the threat posed by the powerful Egyptian artillery that could devastate any attacking formations. To this end, a helicopter-borne force of paratroopers was to be landed some four kilometres (two miles) behind enemy lines at a landing zone codenamed Trapeze and then attack the artillery park from the rear. The mission was given to the 80th Paratroop Brigade commanded by Col. Dani Matt. The scene depicts the assault of the paratroopers (1) against the dug-in Soviet 130mm B-13 artillery pieces (2) while the Sikorsky S-58 helicopters of No. 124 'Rolling Sword' Squadron (3), commanded by Lt. Col .Eliezer 'Cheetah' Cohen, depart the battlefield. As the paratroopers came in from the west, so the three infantry battalions of Col. Kuti Adam's 99th Infantry Brigade each attacked one of the defence lines from the east supported by the M50/M51 Shermans (4) of Col. Mordechai Zippori's 14th Armored Brigade that illuminated the enemy trenchlines with their searchlights. By daybreak the position was subdued but mopping operations continued for much of the morning. It was a remarkable victory at a cost to the Israelis of 40 dead and 140 wounded.

natural defences were further strengthened by the presence of two major forward positions – at Tarat um Basis and Um Tarpe – that lay a little way off to the north-east. Um Katef was further protected by strong fortifications at Ruafa Dam and nearby Quseima, manned by the Egyptian 2nd Infantry Division.

The mission given to Ugda Sharon was to capture this immense stronghold. His *ugda* comprised Colonel Mordechai Zippori's 14th Armored Brigade, Colonel Kuti Adam's 99th Infantry Brigade, Colonel Dani Matt's 80th Paratroop Brigade, and six battalions of artillery (105mm and 155mm howitzers) – not a large force in comparison with the one they were facing. However, they had a great deal of detailed information about the objective because the IDF General Staff had conducted a series of detailed studies of the reasons for their failure in 1956. In addition, before withdrawing in 1957, a team of officers had carefully examined the positions, thoroughly surveying, mapping and photographing every facet of the area. Furthermore, an attack on the Abu Ageila position had become a major map exercise to be considered every year at the IDF Command and Staff College. The exercise had been updated every year in order to include any of the changes that the Egyptians were making. Accordingly Brig. Gen. Sharon, who had been Director of Army Training just prior to the Six Day War, was probably more familiar with the stronghold than anyone else in the IDF. But no number of map exercises can compare with the realities of war.

At 0815hrs on 5 June, Ugda Sharon crossed the frontier in the vicinity of El Auja–Nitzana. The El Auja position had been a UN outpost but it was now deserted. Contact was first made with the enemy at Tarat Um Basis where there was a hilltop outpost including a company of T-34/85 tanks, further protected by a minefield. After an exchange of fire lasting some two hours, the Egyptian garrison withdrew having achieved their mission, namely to delay the Israeli advance. The same happened at the outpost at Um Tarpe but by mid-afternoon the *ugda's* reconnaissance battalion and Zippori's armoured brigade had reached the El Arish–Abu Ageila road in a number of places to the north of the main fortified area. They then established a roadblock to the north-west of Abu Ageila to prevent any enemy reinforcements from El Arish and Bir Lahfan

from interfering. At the same time, AMX-13 light tanks and jeeps, belonging to the reconnaissance battalion also captured a small enemy position at Darb el Turki, which connected the Um Katef position with Quseima. One of the major problems that had to be solved was the fact that a considerable amount of the Israeli artillery was out of range of the main Um Katef position. It was necessary to move it closer in the dark in order to be within range of their targets and thus able to support the night attacks. There were also doubts in Southern Command about whether the *ugda* was sufficiently well trained to undertake the complicated plan that Sharon had devised against the entrenched Egyptian 2nd Infantry Division of some 16,000 men. As the official history comments 'All now depends on the accuracy of the execution by the soldiers and the control by the battle commanders.'

Brigadier-General Sharon's plan for taking the main Abu Ageila–Um Katef positions was indeed complex. First the Centurion battalion of Zippori's 14th Armored Brigade, after crossing an area of sand dunes, would move to envelop the Um Katef–Abu Ageila positions from the north at the same time as his Sherman battalion and the mechanized infantry battalion from the same brigade, carried out an attack on the forward positions of the Um Katef complex. This meant that the Egyptians would be occupied dealing with simultaneous attacks on these areas when Adam's 99th Infantry Brigade launched the main attack. This brigade was to attack across the sand dunes to the north of Um Katef and parallel with the lines of the Egyptian trenches, one infantry battalion being assigned to deal with each of the three lines of trenches that were held by three enemy infantry battalions belonging to the 12th Infantry Brigade of the Egyptian 2nd Infantry Division. The trenches extended over an area five kilometres wide and one kilometre deep and were protected by dense minefields and numerous barbed-wire fences. Strong anti-tank gun positions, dug-in tanks and concrete bunkers, protected the infantry from selected vantage points. As the Israeli infantry advanced along the trench lines, the Shermans would swing round right-handed from the front of the Um Katef position, into the sand dunes and follow behind the infantry, using both their main and secondary armament to boost the envelopment. Immediately behind the Egyptian infantry trenches were six battalions of artillery that also had to be dealt with by the attackers as a priority Further to the west were local reserves including a tank regiment with 66 T-34/85 tanks and a battalion of 22 SU-100 self-propelled guns, to provide a local mobile counterattack reserve; however, their commander did not have the authority to act on his own initiative which was to prove decisive in the coming battle.

The assault was a deliberate night attack. This was for two main reasons: firstly, because it meant that the enemy artillery would be less able to engage their targets with accuracy and secondly that the less well-disciplined Egyptian soldiers would be more likely to become disorganized and suffer a lowering of their morale at night. Both these factors would favour the Israelis. Brigadier-General Sharon had arranged for the infantry battalions of Col. Adam's brigade to be equipped with coloured flashlights – red, green and blue – with which to signal to the tanks, one company of which were assigned to each battalion, so that they could stay in touch as the armour followed the infantry clearing the trenches. Also close behind the infantry were the *ugda*'s combat engineers, clearing a path through the minefields so that the tanks would be able to advance deeper into the position. Whilst the Israeli artillery concentrated their fire on the enemy infantry in the trenches, a battalion of Col. Matt's paratroopers would be carrying out a helicopter assault on the enemy gun lines,

their mission being to neutralize the enemy artillery. Finally, it must be said that Brig. Gen. Sharon had deliberately chosen north as being the direction from which the main assault was to be made, principally because this was an area of sand dunes which the Egyptians had considered impassable, but the careful Israeli terrain studies after the 1956 war, had shown that this was not the case and that both tanks and infantry were able to move through this area, albeit with difficulty. Indeed this was a key element in the success of this daring plan. Another was the totally unprecedented night heliborne attack, aimed at eliminating the major threat posed by the enemy artillery and timed to get under way at last light. The Sikorsky S-58 helicopters of No. 124 Squadron inserted the paratroopers, although half the helicopters got lost in the dark and never found the right landing zone. It was one of the most dramatic actions of the war and the paratroop commander, Col. Dani Matt, recounted the hazardous assault:

Mechanized infantry advance at speed across the trackless Sinai Desert on 6 June 1967. Despite its age, the M3 half-track was well suited to the conditions in the Sinai although fuel consumption and engine wear were high.

> My job was to storm and destroy as many Egyptian artillery guns as we could in the shortest time possible before their armoured reinforcements could come to their rescue. My mission was clear but highly dangerous. Provided we could get away relatively unscathed by landing right in the middle of the enemy defences, we still had to trek a long way to our objective, probably under fire and hauling our heavy loads in total darkness and in uncharted terrain – a piece of cake! Despite the fact that we had landed just a few kilometres from the objective, we were seemingly still undetected. The going in the soft sand was much slower than we had expected and the men tired rapidly, their heavy loads soon becoming almost unbearable, but their officers encouraged them to continue. Suddenly, the sky lit up with hundreds of illumination shells, followed by the crash of explosives as mortar fire landed on our approach route. However, I guessed from the location of falling bombs that the enemy was firing blind, not having actually seen us, only hearing the unfamiliar noise of the helicopters in their rear area. Navigation became difficult in the dark, but as we neared the enemy positions, we could see the artillery gun flashes, which guided us right towards them and soon after midnight, we reached the outer perimeter of the artillery gun area. To my surprise we found that it wasn't even protected by minefields or barbed wire fences, so we stormed

straight in. I had given orders to attack each gun position and they were in a shambles! The gun crews were throwing away their shells, running away in panic, trying to escape our firing. Ammunition bunkers exploded into fiery infernos, the noise became overwhelming, the smoke and dust suffocating. Then, as if by magic, a convoy fully laden with ammunition and with their headlights blazing, came driving right into the battle zone, their drivers completely ignoring what was going on around them. Within seconds they had turned into a blazing inferno, adding to the already chaotic scene in the compound. By now we had almost completed our mission and were busy collecting our dead and wounded, when Gen. Sharon radioed us to return so as to clear the way for the break-in battle, which went ahead according to plan, but without the vicious artillery barrage that we had now eliminated.

In fact the paratroopers had done much more than silence the Egyptian artillery position at Um Katef. They actually helped enormously to bring about the collapse of the entire Abu Ageila complex, by attacking the Egyptians in a crucial and vulnerable position and thus unbalancing their entire defence posture at a critical phase of the battle. Although the helicopter/paratroop operation was highly successful, the troops attacking the frontal area had their problems owing to a shortage of mine-clearing tanks. At Point 181, the Centurion tanks of Colonel Natan 'Natke' Nir's battalion had broken through the rear defences successfully in a wide flanking manoeuvre and stood poised to exploit the situation. Meanwhile, the Israeli artillery that had moved well forward during the late afternoon and had managed to register onto a number of important checkpoints before it got too dark. At 2200hrs, six battalions of artillery unleashed the greatest bombardment in Israeli history with 6,000 rounds being fired on Um Katef following Brig. Gen. Sharon's pronouncement 'Let everything tremble.' The guns poured heavy fire onto the Egyptian trenches for over 20 minutes, whilst the Egyptian artillery, reeling under the paratroop attack, was unable to reply, thus allowing the assaulting forces to cross the start line relatively unhindered. While Zippori's brigade carried out its diversionary actions, Col. Adam's infantry advanced on the Um Katef main positions from the north. The first battalion under Lieutenant-Colonel Dov hit the first trench, the second under Lieutenant-Colonel Ofer David took on the second trench and the third under Lieutenant-Colonel Kastel assaulted the third as planned. At the same time, the Shermans turned in behind them and began firing over their heads down onto the trenches that they were assaulting.

Meanwhile at the rear of the enemy positions, the paratroopers had completed their mission successfully – the enemy artillery was neutralized, much of its ammunition destroyed, many of their vehicles knocked out and the gun crews separated from their guns. Having caused chaos all round, the paratroopers withdrew, as they knew that the next stage of the assault would see the Centurion battalion advancing from the north and thus it was essential for them not to be in their line of fire. Nir's Centurions had in fact reached the El Arish–Abu Ageila road at last light, codenamed *Oakland* on IDF maps, and then waited there for H-Hour. When the fighting broke out to the south of them, they advanced and neutralized the Abu Ageila strongpoint. They then bypassed the crossroads and pressed on southwards towards the heart of the Egyptian position. Sharon's carefully coordinated plan called for them to be met there by the Sherman battalion, the two then being ready to deal with any Egyptian counterattack. In the 1956 war, this had been one of their failures at Abu Ageila when there had been an encounter between two Israeli tank units – each had thought that the other was the enemy, with devastating effects.

By 0330hrs, the Shermans, which had been delayed by minefields and other obstacles, now gallantly dealt with by the *ugda's* engineer battalion, were finally able to break through the Um Katef position and approach their anticipated meeting point with the other battalion. At the same time Col. Zippori started to receive radio messages from his two battalion commanders that they were both under heavy fire and were responding. Zippori immediately ordered the Sherman battalion to cease firing so that they would be able to determine whether or not they were firing at each other by mistake. The Centurion battalion continued to receive fire so clearly both were being shot at by the enemy and not by each other. In fact the Egyptians had moved up some reserve tanks in an attempt to restore the contested positions. There followed a confused, fierce tank battle in the pitch darkness. The two Israeli tank battalions now able to coordinate their efforts against a common enemy. They soon were gaining the upper hand when, out of the blue appeared another column of tanks from the north-east which drove south-west from the Abu Ageila crossroads and into the desert. After a brief exchange of fire, it was quickly realized that this column was from the armoured brigade of Colonel Elhanan Sela of Ugda Yoffe that was moving to intercept the Egyptian 4th Armoured Division. By dawn the defences of Abu Ageila–Um Katef were broken with long convoys of Egyptian vehicles fleeing westwards, soon to become hapless victims of the marauding IAF now that Operation *Moked* was complete. For Ugda Sharon, much of the next day was taken up with consolidating the battlefield and neutralizing the extensive defence works of Abu Ageila–Um Katef. It was a stunning victory over the strongest Egyptian position in the Sinai; as Brig. Gen. Sharon noted at one point 'It was all working like a Swiss watch.' By now the 7th and 200th armored brigades had linked up to form a pocket containing the remnants of the Egyptian formations in north-eastern Sinai; the 4th Armoured Division had been given a bloody nose; Abu Ageila had fallen; Force Shazli was isolated to the south while the reconnaissance group of Ugda Tal was racing along the coastal road towards the Suez Canal. The campaign was now ahead of schedule and the IDF needed to take some major decisions about how to proceed after the breakthrough phase, as indeed did the Egyptian Army.

A column of M50 Shermans churns across the central sector of the Sinai Desert on the second day of the war. The M50 Sherman was fitted with a 75mm CN75-50 high-velocity gun similar to that mounted in the AMX-13 light tank, together with a Cummins V8 460hp diesel engine for increased range and battlefield survivability.

The Sinai front

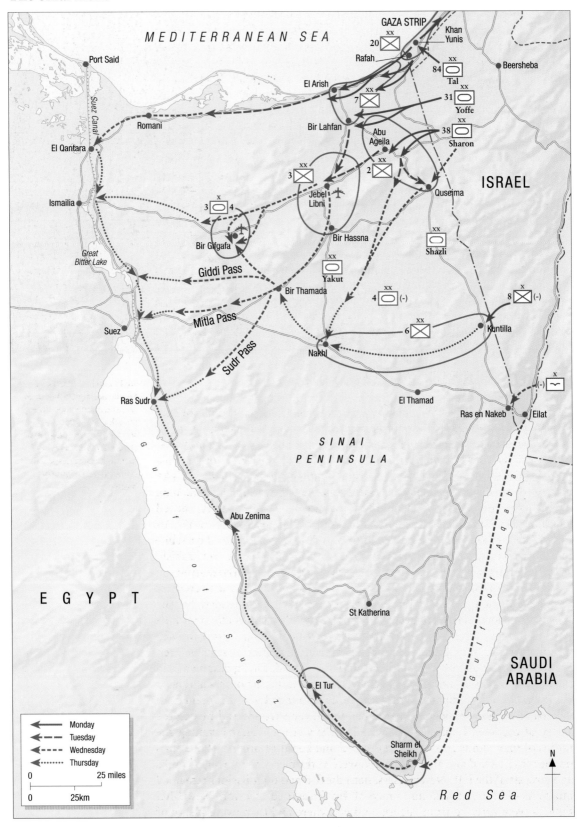

MEDITERRANEAN SEA

Port Said

GAZA STRIP

Khan Yunis

20 (xx)

Rafah

Beersheba

84 Tal (xx)

El Arish

7 (xx)

31 Yoffe (xx)

Romani

Bir Lahfan

38 Sharon (xx)

Abu Ageila

El Qantara

Suez Canal

ISRAEL

3 (xx)

2 (xx)

Ismailia

Jebel Libni

Quseima

3 x 4

Great Bitter Lake

Bir Gifgafa

Bir Hassna

Shazli (xx)

Giddi Pass

Yakut (xx)

Bir Thamada

4 (xx) (-)

8 x (-)

Mitla Pass

6 (xx)

Kuntilla

Suez

Sudr Pass

Nakhl

Ras Sudr

El Thamad

(-) x

Ras en Nakeb

Eilat

SINAI PENINSULA

EGYPT

Gulf of Suez

Abu Zenima

St Katherina

SAUDI ARABIA

Gulf of Aqaba

El Tur

x

Sharm el Sheikh

	Monday
	Tuesday
	Wednesday
	Thursday

0   25 miles

0   25km

N

Red Sea

70

THE OTHER SIDE OF THE HILL

By the late afternoon of 5 June, the Egyptian high command and political leadership finally realized the enormity of what had befallen the Egyptian Air Force. Nevertheless, euphoric radio broadcasts of 'The Voice of the Arabs' continued across the Arab world with outrageous claims of victory against the 'Zionist entity' – Tel Aviv had been bombed; 80 per cent of the IAF destroyed; the oil storage depots at Haifa ablaze; the Egyptian and Jordanian armies were advancing to meet each other in the Negev Desert, indeed triumph over Israel was at hand. On hearing of the destruction of the air force, a shattered Nasser hid in his home and did not emerge for days while refusing to see any visitors. Sadat retired into a stupor of whisky and hashish. By the morning of 6 June, Field Marshal Amer had learned of the destruction of his two forward divisions and the crushing defeat of the seemingly impregnable defences of Abu Ageila–Um Katef. Overwhelmed by the disastrous reports, a distraught Amer issued a general order for all units in the Sinai to retreat to the Gidi and Mitla passes in western Sinai, just 32km (20 miles) from the Suez Canal. He did not consult his chief of staff or even President Nasser. Already demoralized and disoriented, the Egyptian units in the Sinai began their disorganized retreat. Again conflicting orders and poor communications hampered every move compounded by the premature departure of many officers as they abandoned their troops and fled to the safety of the Suez Canal. By now the Israelis were routinely jamming the radios of many units leaving them isolated and bereft of orders. Those units on the move lacked any air support and were at the mercy of rampaging tanks and aircraft of the IDF. Nevertheless, both the 3rd and 6th divisions remained intact, as did Force Shazli and much of 4th Armoured Division. New MiG fighters were arriving from Algeria and elsewhere and there were plenty of

Tanks and half-tracks of Ugda Sharon are replenished with fuel and ammunition during the advance across the southern sector of the Sinai Desert. The wide variety of AFVs in IDF service gave rise to serious logistical supply problems.

A medic rushes to the aid of injured tank crewmen as they evacuate their stricken M48A2C Patton. Each man shows the effects of flash burns on their bare arms and faces. Israeli tank commanders commonly fought their tanks with their heads exposed out of the turret. In consequence, they suffered a disproportionate number of casualties during the war.

pilots to fly them. Realizing the magnitude of the problem, the Egyptian High Command rescinded Amer's retreat order but this only added to the confusion. Now was the time to seek an immediate ceasefire at the United Nations through the Soviet Union before these unfortunate defeats turned to disaster. With Cairo Radio declaring victory after victory, it would have been political suicide for Nasser to take such an action. However, the Soviet Union saw no cause for concern since it was being fed the same lies and proclaimed in an official statement 'its resolute support and complete confidence' in the Arab nations' 'just struggle against Imperialism and Zionism'. In Washington DC, the Johnson administration was under no illusions about the progress of the war. In a memo to the President, National Security Advisor Walt Rostow advised, 'Herewith the account, with a map, of the first day's turkey shoot.'

UGDA YOFFE, 6 JUNE

The first 'enemy' to be encountered by Ugda Yoffe as it crossed into the Sinai on 5 June were the treacherous sand dunes of the Wadi Haridin; an area considered as impassable by the Egyptians ever since the 1956 war. However, as stated above, Col. Yissacher Shadmi's 200th Armored Brigade had already successfully penetrated these 'impassable' sand dunes and had been able to surprise the enemy in the Bir Lahfan area and subdue the strongholds of Bir Hassna and Bir Thamada, thus sealing the Egyptian lines of retreat from north-eastern Sinai. The role of Ugda Yoffe was to penetrate as deeply as possible into the enemy positions in central Sinai in order to forestall any enemy counterattacks that might be mounted against the other two *ugdas* of Tal and Sharon, thus enabling them to complete their breakthrough operations and leave the way clear to begin the next phase of operations, namely the penetration of the Egyptian second line and the destruction of their armoured forces while, at the same time, preventing them from escaping through the passes and over the Suez Canal. Blocking these passes would mean that all enemy forces east of the Canal would effectively be trapped. As the official history states: 'The commanders knew that the attainment of their objective depends upon speed, ensured fuel supply, resourcefulness, and stubborn fighting by every tank crew. … The Task Force sets off at an incredible pace. It becomes an obstacle race against an enemy determined at all costs to get through the passes and cross the Canal.'

Late in the afternoon of 6 June, elements of the 200th Armored Brigade were approaching the Egyptian position at Jebel Libni from Bir Lahfan. They reached the defensive minefields in front of the enemy position and came under fire from Egyptian tanks at long range. Tanks swiftly deployed off

TOP
The fleet of modified Shermans was the most numerous tank in the IDF inventory during the Six Day War with 522 of them in service in June 1967. Of these, 180 were the more powerful M51 Sherman armed with the French 105mm smoothbore gun that was capable of destroying modern Soviet tanks such as the T-54 and T-55. These M51 Shermans of the 14th Armored Brigade, part of Ugda Sharon, are shown on exercise in the Negev desert prior to the war.

BOTTOM
Israeli soldiers dive for cover as a pair of MiG-17 fighters strafes a convoy of trucks on the approaches to the Suez Canal on 9 June 1967. In spite of Operation *Moked*, the Egyptian Air Force was soon reinforced by aircraft from Algeria and elsewhere. These were quickly pressed into service and flew combat missions up to the end of the war.

the road, as did those of the 7th Armored Brigade that was following them. Both brigades prepared to envelop the Egyptian camp. They were joined soon afterwards by Brig. Gen. Yoffe's other brigade under Col. Elhanan Sela that had motored down the Abu Ageila road from a bivouac position just west of Abu Ageila. The battle for the Jebel Libni position started at last light and continued in the darkness. Two enemy armoured brigades were entrenched there – the 141st and the elite Egyptian 'Palace Guard', the latter equipped with modern Soviet T-55 tanks. The Israeli tanks approached with care, opening fire at maximum range, one battalion moving around the enemy positions to outflank them while a second battalion attacked head-on. A fierce battle ensued, as the Israeli tanks stormed into both the camp and the airfield, eventually putting the enemy to flight. The Egyptians lost some 30 tanks in this desperate rearguard action, but they did manage to hold up the Israelis for several hours. Under cover of darkness, the remnants of the Egyptian rearguard then withdrew westwards towards Bir Hamma. The three Israeli brigade commanders all decided to let their exhausted troops rest and regroup so did not resume the offensive until after dawn on 7 June.

THE RACE FOR THE PASSES

Late on 6 June, Brig. Gen. Gavish called his three *ugda* commanders – Tal, Sharon and Yoffe – to his forward command post for a conference. The situation was now becoming clear with the Egyptian withdrawal turning into a headlong retreat and if the Israelis did not act swiftly enough, the bulk of the Egyptian forces would escape from Sinai and withdraw over the Suez Canal to safety. This had to be prevented at all costs and called for an unorthodox method of pursuit, which he then outlined. Each of the two northern *ugdas* of Tal and Yoffe would send armoured spearheads westwards along the three central Sinai roads, pushing forwards with all speed, endeavouring to ignore or bypass any enemy they met en route. They would then establish roadblocks in the vicinity of Bir Gifgafa, the Giddi Pass and the Mitla Pass. The residue of their forces, together with Sharon's *ugda*, would then advance on a broad front, driving the enemy westwards onto the waiting roadblocks, followed by maximum destruction from both land and air.

On their return to their own command posts, they agreed the following steps: firstly, Tal's 'roadblock' force would take the northern route through Bir Gifgafa and block the road to Ismailia; Yoffe's would take the southern route and block both the Mitla and Giddi passes. The 7th Armored Brigade would, as usual, be the spearhead of Ugda Tal, whilst 200th Armored Brigade would lead Ugda Yoffe; the remainder of both *ugdas* would then follow in a rapid but deliberate advance in line with Brig. Gen. Gavish's orders. Having radioed their proposals to Gavish and received his approval, they prepared once again for action and gave out their orders to their brigade commanders.

At first light, countless enemy vehicles of all types were crawling westwards in headlong retreat. A battalion of Centurions of Ugda Yoffe was ordered to reach the Mitla Pass and seal it before they escaped. However, most of the Israeli tanks were running short of fuel and all that the Centurion battalion commander, Lieutenant-Colonel Bar-Am, could muster was just 12 runners. Nevertheless, he set off with this small party to take on the Egyptians who still had a force of over 600 operational tanks. Overtaking any enemy tanks in their path, Bar-Am's force smashed its way through all enemy opposition, including

a strong position at the Parker Memorial crossroads, which had been the scene of the 890th Paratroop Battalion's gallant action in the 1956 War. They reached the pass with their last drops of fuel – four of his small band already having to be towed into action, their gas tanks empty. They immediately set up an ambush. Then good fortune reigned as a small group of Israeli armoured infantry and self-propelled artillery arrived, thus considerably strengthening the ambush position. Providentially, they were carrying some spare fuel with them so were able to replenish Bar-Am's empty gas tanks. And not a moment too soon as close on their heels came the first Egyptian column. All that night the battle raged as the enemy columns tried desperately to smash their way through, but to no avail. In the morning, the IAF arrived and once again, devastated the Egyptian forces as first hundreds, then thousands of burning vehicles blocked the approaches to the pass.

On the northern route Ugda Tal continued their advance, fighting several armoured battles with enemy tanks that tried to block their way. With 7th Armored Brigade still in the lead, the divisional vanguard approached Bir Gifgafa airfield during late afternoon, as reports were coming in that the Egyptian 4th Armoured Division was moving north. Deciding to engage, Brig. Gen. Tal sent his reserve 60th Armored Brigade west while turning the 7th south to meet the enemy in a two-pronged attack. The 7th placed a strong anvil of tanks while manoeuvring a hammer to turn the enemy flank. However, the enemy tanks did not seek battles and retreated further south.

Colonel Menachem Aviram's 60th Armored Brigade had now taken over from 7th Armored, leading the *ugda* and was encountering retreating Egyptian units going westwards. The Israelis went around them, drove them off the road or pushed through them in a series of bizarre running battles. By afternoon, they had reached the road junction north of Bir Gifgafa. Aviram then sent Lieutenant-Colonel Zeev Eitan's 19th Light Tank Battalion, equipped with AMX-13 light tanks, to the west, ordering them to take up a defensive position

TOP
A formation of Centurions is loaded with ammunition prior to the war. These tanks are armed with the L7 105mm gun that proved to be an outstanding weapon when firing armour-piercing discarding sabot ammunition that became the scourge of Arab tank units.

BOTTOM
Israeli soldiers of Ugda Tal observe an artillery bombardment of Egyptian positions in the northern sector of the Sinai close to the Suez Canal on 8 June 1967. The vehicles are M38A10 jeeps mounting the M40 106mm recoilless rifle; the standard equipment of reconnaissance units, combining high mobility and sufficient firepower to engage enemy armour in an emergency.

in the hills just beyond Bir Gifgafa, blocking the road from Ismailia. Around midnight, their position would be the scene of a fierce tank battle, when an Egyptian armoured brigade from Ismailia that had been sent to reinforce 4th Armoured Division but not knowing that much of the division had already withdrawn to the canal, blundered into the roadblock. The Israelis had a good position on the outer rim of a semicircle of small hills, facing west. Their fuel, ammunition and supplies were in half-tracks in a central position to the rear. They had the advantage of being in a prepared defensive position but they comprised a force of only some 15 15-ton light AMX-13 tanks, while the Egyptian formation numbered some 50–60 T-54 and T-55 medium tanks. Two enemy trucks had first entered the roadblock, were fired on and their crews killed or taken prisoner. Then the noise of heavy tank engines was heard from the west, along the road from Ismailia and a little while later the leading enemy tank appeared. The diminutive AMX-13s engaged the enemy with their 75mm guns but saw their armour-piercing shells bounce off the T-55s frontal armour

THE RACE TO THE MITLA PASS, 7 JUNE 1967 (pp. 78–79)

By the third day of the war, the Egyptian units in the Sinai were in full retreat and, in the early hours of Wednesday morning, the first Israeli forces reached the Suez Canal. To ensure that the Egyptian forces did not retire to fight another day, it was essential to block the various mountain passes that formed the only exits from the Sinai to the Suez Canal and safety. The task of sealing the Mitla and Giddi passes was given to the 200th Armored Brigade commanded by Col. Yissacher Shadmi. He in turn ordered forwards his Centurion battalion under the command of Lt. Col. Abraham Bar-Am. The brigade was desperately short of fuel and Bar-Am set off from Bir Thamada with just 12 tanks. By the time the armoured column reached the Parker Memorial, a curious British landmark some 24km (15 miles) east of the Mitla Pass, only four tanks were motoring under their own power while four that had run out of fuel were being towed by others. With enemy vehicles and tanks on all sides, the small force of Centurions (1) charged down the narrow tarmac road towards their goal while

Vautour IIA ground attack aircraft (2) of the No. 110 'Knights of the Heart' Squadron operating out of Tel Nof airbase kept the enemy at bay. As the sun was setting, just nine Centurions finally reached the mouth of the pass where hundreds of Egyptian vehicles were burning following repeated attacks by the IAF. There they formed a circular defensive position on a flat-topped knoll with a battery of AMX 105mm self-propelled guns and some infantrymen in M3 half-tracks. The first Egyptian attack of 22 T-54s was beaten off without loss. Throughout the night, the battle raged in the glare of burning vehicles but the pass was blocked and no Egyptian tank escaped the guns of the Centurions. By 0800hrs on Thursday morning, the battle was over with the exhausted tankers slumped at their crew positions. Not a single Centurion was lost although one had been hit 12 times by direct-fire weapons. Just one infantryman had been killed and four others wounded. The fate of the Egyptian Army in the Sinai was now sealed.

while the enemy heavier tank guns replied, knocking out some of the Israeli unit's half-tracks and light tanks with ease. One of these was laden with ammunition and exploded, which then set off a chain reaction destroying a further seven half-tracks and a tank, killing 16 Israelis. The battle continued with the much lighter Israeli tanks faring badly, until the CO personally led some of his tanks off to a flank to engage the thinner side armour of the enemy AFVs. The battle had lasted for some two hours when, eventually, the light tanks were forced to withdraw for want of fuel and ammunition. Fortunately at this time, a battalion of upgraded M51 Sherman tanks, mounting the 105mm L/44 gun, arrived to even up the odds. It had the desired result and soon a number of enemy tanks were in flames, their crews bailing out and rushing away while the remainder withdrew in confusion back towards the canal. Colonel Aviram had also successfully blocked the road to Bir Thamada so both routes were blocked. Meanwhile, 7th Armored Brigade, having regrouped after their latest encounter, was now close behind Aviram. Approaching the Bir Gifgafa road junction, it turned southwards, hoping to encircle what was left of the Egyptian 4th Armoured Division that had been concentrated in the Bir Gifgafa area but only the Egyptian 3rd Armoured Brigade and some stragglers remained as the rest of the division had escaped towards the Suez Canal.

Ugda Yoffe was also having much the same experiences although theirs included even more serious enemy pressure. The 200th Armored Brigade had moved off at 0400hrs towards Bir Hassna and at first light ran into the Egyptian rearguard in a strongly fortified area. The leading battalion attacked the position while the other two battalions bypassed the enemy and reached the Bir Thamada road to the south-west of Bir Hassna. By 0900hrs they had taken the enemy position and moved on, leaving Col. Sela's brigade that was following to mop up. With Bir Thamada deserted, Col. Shadmi divided his brigade there, sending one battalion to block the Giddi Pass and one to block

The battles for the Gidi and Mitla passes were hard and bitter as the remnants of the Egyptian Army retreated westwards through the narrow defiles. Cruelly exposed to Israeli airpower and armoured formations, the Egyptians suffered horrendous casualties.

the Mitla Pass. The former had a fairly simple time, overrunning groups of Egyptian stragglers, reaching the pass safely and setting up their roadblock. They then held off a number of Egyptian units that tried to get through during the afternoon and evening.

The situation at the Mitla Pass was vastly different, mainly because of the sheer numbers of enemy vehicles trying to escape. There were so many more Egyptian vehicles to get round, or fight through, thus not only holding up their armour, but also delaying their supply vehicles that were carrying their vital first line fuel and ammunition – some of these vehicles having been knocked out by enemy fire, whilst others were broken down. Shadmi's tanks were therefore running out of fuel when they were still over 19km (12 miles) from the pass. They had to resort, as Lt. Col. Bar-Am had done on the northern route, to towing their breakdowns or, *in extremis*, abandoning them. It was almost 1800hrs before Shadmi's diminutive force reached the eastern end of the pass. He had just nine tanks – five runners and four being towed, with which to establish his roadblock. A short distance behind were a handful of half-tracks carrying some mechanized infantry and mortars. With this small party he set up his roadblock and caught the first Egyptian tanks that were following immediately behind him completely by surprise. One observer commented, 'The tide of Egyptian vehicles continued to flow to the pass. As they converged on the entrance to the defile, just east of Shadmi's ambush position, the Israeli Air Force strafed and bombed them with high explosive, rockets and napalm. Hundreds, then thousands of vehicles were soon piled up in the area, leaving little room for manoeuvre.' The pressure on Shadmi's small band was now immense and by 2000hrs he reported to Yoffe that he was completely surrounded and cut off. The *ugda* commander immediately ordered Col. Sela's brigade (back near Bir Thamada) to refuel and then to rush to Shadmi's assistance, adding that he must endeavour to arrive at the pass by 0300hrs at the latest. The relief column set off without lights, and in the pitch dark one sub-unit got itself hopelessly entangled with a column of enemy tanks that did not appear to realize that they were Israeli. The Israeli tanks continued along with the enemy until the

IDF 105mm self-propelled guns based on the AMX-13 chassis bombard Egyptian positions along the Suez Canal on 9 June 1967. The IDF was woefully lacking in self-propelled artillery during the war and the ground forces were obliged to seek assistance from the air force to provide much-needed direct fire support.

commander sent out an order over the radio for all his tanks to turn right off the road, halt and switch on their searchlights, then fire at any tank that was still on the road. In this manner they not only untangled themselves, but also knocked out an entire Egyptian tank battalion within moments. Shadmi's brave little force held out through the night, despite being reduced to scavenging the battlefield for enemy guns and ammunition when theirs ran out; however, by early morning even that source had dried up. Fortunately, Sela's relief party was approaching, arriving at first light and the Egyptians, realizing that they were now caught between the two groups of Israelis tanks, began to abandon their vehicles and set off on foot into the desert.

ON TO THE CANAL

Ugda Sharon was now advancing from east to west, driving the enemy onto the other *ugdas*' ambush positions like beaters on a pheasant shoot. Progress had been slow because of the difficult terrain and the presence of Egyptian minefields. Resistance was sporadic while other units collapsed completely, such as the Egyptian 125th Armoured Brigade that abandoned all its SU-100 self-propelled guns without a fight. Later the Israelis captured the commander of the unit and quizzed him about his actions. His extraordinary explanation was that he had initially been alarmed to hear the approach of tanks during the night of 6/7 June that he had taken to be enemy although they turned out to be friendly. He then received orders to retreat and decided to abandon his AFVs and withdraw with his tank crews in APCs. He made for Bir Thamada only to find that it was held by the Israelis so he next abandoned his tank crews, leaving them in total disarray, and then, with two other officers, headed off south-west hoping to reach the canal and safety. Soon afterwards he was captured by an Israeli patrol and when asked why he had not destroyed his tanks explained that, while the orders had told him to withdraw, they had not said anything about destroying his tanks. In any case, he had added, the noise

As the Cinderella service of the IDF, the Israeli Navy played only a small part in the Sinai campaign of the Six Day War. The Navy's main role was to defend the Israeli coastline from incursion and maintain open sea lanes so that ships carrying vital military equipment and ammunition could dock in Israeli ports throughout the war. Its most significant military operation was the capture of Sharm el Sheikh at the southern tip of the Sinai Peninsula, as shown here with supplies being unloaded on the beaches from a landing craft on 7 June 1967.

The crew of an M3 half-track take time to rest and recuperate on the banks of the Suez Canal on 9 June 1967 with the Firdan swing bridge in the background. The array of radio antennae indicates that this is a command vehicle.

would have given his position away to the enemy. It was an all too familiar tale about the Egyptian officer corps. The Egyptian Army was now in complete disarray. Confusion led to collapse. In the words of a driver of the 6th Mechanized Division, Mahmud al-Suwarqa:

> We were waiting to carry out our orders and advance on Eilat when suddenly on 7 June both the company and battalion commanders disappeared. Later I found out that they fled over the canal. I abandoned my jeep and joined a column retreating to Nakhl where we were exposed to aerial attack. Then at the Mitla Pass we ran into Israelis who appeared to be coming from Suez. They fired shells and machine guns at us and after that I felt nothing. I awoke in an Israeli vehicle soaked in my own blood.

Early on 8 June, Brig. Gen. Sharon's 14th Armored Brigade reached Nakhl and then came the news that Colonel Mendler's 8th Armored Brigade, which had been operating independently further south, had just taken El Thamad and driven off the garrison – comprising an infantry brigade supported by a tank brigade – in the direction of Nakhl. Harassing the rearguard of this enemy force was one of Mendler's tank battalions. Sharon quickly put his two tank battalions into ambush positions just to the east of Nakhl and awaited the arrival of the Egyptian 6th Mechanized Division. Soon a major tank battle was under way, Sharon personally taking a mechanized infantry battalion into the middle of the Egyptian column. By mid-afternoon it was all over. Between this part of Ugda Sharon and Mendler's leading battalion, they had destroyed some 60 enemy tanks, 100 assorted guns and over 300 vehicles of all types. Several hundred Egyptians had been killed or wounded, whilst some 5,000 had fled into the surrounding desert. The battle of Nakhl over, Sharon's forces regrouped and continued on westerly to link up with Yoffe's *ugda* near Bir Thamada.

Meanwhile, down in the far south of the Sinai Peninsula, preparations were under way to mount a combined land and sea attack on Sharm el Sheikh. On 7 June, a force of paratroops prepared to fly from Eilat while a small naval force of three motor torpedo boats carefully made its way through the Straits of Tiran, which it discovered had not been mined. They landed at the Egyptian coastal base and found it deserted since the Egyptian garrison had joined the general retreat. As the paratroop force overflew Sharm el Sheikh, they realized the Egyptians had fled so, instead of making an operational jump, landed on the airstrip, finding that the navy was already in residence. Thereafter the paratroopers moved off north-westwards along the coast, reaching El Tur by last light, where they dug in and waited for further orders. Later they would link up with Yoffe's forces from Ras Sudr.

There had also been another Israeli attack into Sinai as well as the three main *ugdas'* operations and this had taken place on the very first day of the war. The thrust was in the south across the border at Kuntilla and was carried out by Col. Albert Mendler's independent 8th Armored Brigade. The brigade had been deliberately showing its tanks and troops in the days preceding war in order to attract Egyptian attention to the southern area. This was achieved with the deployment of Force Shazli in the area. On the morning of 5 June, Mendler's brigade swept across the border and by early afternoon had breached the defences around Kuntilla. Mendler then sent patrols down the road to Thamad and Nakhl, whilst the major part of the brigade remained in Kuntilla, continuing to pose a threat to the Egyptians. According to Egyptian history their forces at Kuntilla had in fact put up a valiant fight and the action was reported by one of their officers as follows: 'The battalion placed ambushes for the advancing enemy forces which outnumbered us in quantity and firing capacity. ... They confronted them fearlessly and hit a number of Israeli tanks. Only three Egyptian tanks remained and one of these was damaged. Most of the officers and soldiers were killed. I watched my battalion disintegrate ... I saw the bodies of soldiers after the Israeli tanks had run them over ... I saw the wounded lying on the ground utterly unable to help them.' Another eyewitness, who had tried to attack the Israeli Sherman tanks with hand-held rocket-propelled grenades (Russian RPGs) recalled:

> I lay down waiting for a tank. When it was in range I fired, but the weapon did not work. The whole area was turning into hell. Another soldier's RPG didn't work and the tank came at him shooting. He ran at the tank carrying the RPG. The tank squashed him. ... They fired machine guns and more soldiers fell ... I tried the RPG again and it still didn't work. I was in total shock to see my group torn to pieces after we had fought so bravely.

In the final analysis the decoy operations conducted by the 8th Armored Brigade played a major part in the success of the Israeli operations as a whole. They caused the Egyptians to carry out a major redeployment of their armour to the south-eastern region prior to the main Israeli offensive being launched and its continual presence also made them keep this armour well away from the other battlefields to the north until it was far too late for them to influence the eventual outcome. Thus this tactic not only removed a substantial amount of

A mechanized infantry unit approaches an Egyptian military encampment in southern Sinai along one of the few paved roads in the area on 9 June 1967.

armour from the forces initially facing Tal's and Sharon's *ugda*s, but also made them continue to do so until it was far too late. It was estimated that the 60 Sherman tanks of the 8th Armored Brigade held almost 300 Egyptian tanks hostage for a most critical period of the campaign. Afterwards, the 8th Armored Brigade was transferred to the Golan front, involving them in a long and gruelling drive of nearly 350km (220 miles) from their positions in the Negev.

On the morning of 7 June, a force from Ugda Tal under Col. Yisrael Granit reached the eastern edge of the Suez Canal near El Qantara, having made a rapid march along the northern coastal road. He reported his arrival to Brig. Gen. Tal, who then relayed it to General Staff Headquarters at Tel Aviv. The Minister for Defense, Gen. Moshe Dayan, immediately ordered him to withdraw some 19km (12 miles) from the canal with the words, 'I will personally court-martial any Israeli commander who touches the banks of the canal.' But the military imperative of completing the destruction of the Egyptian Army meant that an arbitrary stop line some 19km (12 miles) from the canal was not feasible. Under heavy pressure from Maj. Gen. Rabin, Moshe Dayan relented and allowed the troops to resume the advance. The following morning Granit received more orders, allowing him to move westwards again from Romani. About ten kilometres (six miles) east of El Qantara, they encountered an enemy force of Egyptian commandos with tank support. The engagement that followed lasted some hours, several Egyptian tanks were knocked out and the remainder withdrew back to the canal in the El Qantara area. Early on 9 June, Col. Granit moved forwards again, bypassing El Qantara to a position opposite Ismailia. Later that morning they were joined by elements of the 7th Armored Brigade that had spearheaded the *ugda*'s advance from Bir Gifgafa

The planning for the capture of Sharm el Sheikh was designated Operation *Lights* and was to be a joint operation between paratroopers dropped by the IAF and a landing of commandos from the sea by the Navy once it had breached the Egyptian defences in the Straits of Tiran. In the event, there was little opposition and, much to the consternation of the paratroopers, the Navy got there first. Accordingly, there were no parachute assaults during the war and the paratroopers were landed at Sharm el Sheikh in their Nord Atlas transport aircraft, shown here being unloaded during a sandstorm.

at first light and fought a number of tank battles with Egyptian T-55s, resulting in casualties on both sides, the Israelis then pushing steadily forwards until Col. Gonen's spearhead had joined up with Granit's.

Meanwhile, further south Col. Sela's brigade had managed to push its way through the vast numbers of knocked-out enemy vehicles now blocking the Mitla Pass only to find their way blocked once again, this time by a series of enemy strongpoints, each of which had to be destroyed in place. After some while, Sela pulled his forces back to the pass and made them rest until last light. They then advanced again with lights and guns blazing, this tactic unnerving their opponents, although resistance was stiff. In the early hours of 9 June, Col. Sela's leading troops reached the Suez Canal opposite Shallufa and captured a complete air defence base containing nine undamaged SA-2 anti-aircraft missiles. In addition, Col Shadmi's brigade was also on the move westwards through the passes and by dawn had reached the southern end of the Little Bitter Lake and the canal to the south.

Part of Sela's brigade then moved south-west from the Mitla Pass and soon after midnight reached Ras Sudr on the Gulf of Suez. Shortly after Sela's tanks entered the town, a paratroop force was dropped that linked up with the tanks and together then pushed on southwards along the road running along the eastern side of the Gulf of Suez. At El Tur, they joined up with the force of paratroopers that had moved up there from Sharm el Sheikh. With the exception of the marshes east of Port Fouad, the entire Sinai Peninsula was now in Israeli hands. At 2135hrs on 9 June, the Egyptian representative at the United Nations in New York formally and unconditionally accepted the ceasefire that brought an end to the Sinai campaign.

AFTERMATH – *AL-NAXA*

It was a lightning war: the apogee of blitzkrieg in a stunning campaign of armoured warfare closely integrated with tactical airpower of jet fighter-bombers and close support aircraft. Egyptian casualties in the five days of fighting, according to their official statistics, were some 10,000 men; many of whom died in the desert of thirst or heat exhaustion during the disastrous retreat. The Israelis lost 338 killed and almost 1,400 wounded in the Sinai campaign. The Israelis also captured some 500 officers and over 5,000 men, half of whom were wounded. Nasser later admitted that the Egyptian army lost 80 per cent of its equipment in the Sinai including 700 tanks, with 100 of them taken intact and undamaged by the Israelis, whose losses in tanks were just 122. They also destroyed or captured 400 field guns of Russian origin, 50 self-propelled guns, 30 heavy 155mm guns and approximately 10,000 trucks and other assorted vehicles. All these losses in *matériel* were replaced within months by the Soviet Union. Manpower losses amounted to little more than one month's draft of conscripts. The failure of the officer corps was more serious with many senior commanders court-martialled and dismissed.

By any standards, the Third Arab-Israeli War was a staggering defeat for Egypt and the Arab world, a defeat that was the result of the foolhardy strategy

To the victor the spoils – an Israeli infantryman tries his hand at fishing in the Suez Canal. Despite the emphatic military victory of the Six Day War, peace did not prevail and within weeks hostilities resumed along the banks of the international waterway culminating in the War of Attrition that lasted until August 1970. Even so that was just the prelude to the resumption of open conflict with the Yom Kippur War in October 1973.

The Egyptian Government of Gamal Abd el Nasser sued for peace on 9 June 1967. In just five days, 80 per cent of the Egyptian Army was lost in the Sinai Peninsula. Vast amounts of equipment littered the desert and passes for years to come, although the Israelis retrieved any military vehicles and weapons that were intact or repairable and incorporated them into the IDF.

of brinkmanship adopted by President Nasser in his attempt to bolster Syria against Israel. The absolute defeat was compounded by the devious machinations of the Soviet Union and the appalling ineptitude of Field Marshal Amer. Once close friends, Amer and Nasser had become bitter rivals that had split the armed forces into two mutually antagonistic cliques. By 1967, Amer was in the ascendancy. His influence over the armed forces was such that Nasser was denied any knowledge of its real capabilities. In the event, these were critically compromised after the success of the IAF's pre-emptive strike. Amer's catalogue of incompetence knew no bounds, culminating in the disastrous order for a general retreat when over 50 per cent of the formations in the Sinai were still intact. On 9 June, President Nasser proffered his resignation. In spontaneous demonstrations, the Egyptian people rejected this outright. Even so, Nasser's position both at home and abroad was severely weakened. There had to be a scapegoat. Fearing a coup by the armed forces, Nasser was forced to move against his old friend Field Marshal Abd el Hakim Amer. The latter died in suspicious circumstances, reputedly by his own hand but possibly murdered. Yet this was not enough as it revealed only that Nasser had dreadful judgement in his appointment of an incompetent commander-in-chief of the army. The answer lay in the 'big lie'. It was inconceivable that the IAF could have inflicted such a humiliating defeat so the 'Arab street' was told that the air attacks were undertaken by the imperialist powers of America and Britain flying from aircraft carriers in the Mediterranean Sea and from bases in Cyprus. Nasser's fragile

This extraordinary photograph was taken from an IAF helicopter and shows three Egyptian soldiers wandering aimlessly in the burning, waterless wilderness of the Sinai Desert. Egyptian casualties in the Sinai campaign were some 10,000 men while the IDF lost 338 killed and 1,400 wounded.

health was broken by the war and he died on 28 September 1970. His funeral, with its ten-kilometre (six-mile) cortège, attended by seven million people, was possibly the largest in history. Ironically, his 'big lie' helped to cement the lasting commitment of the United States to the state of Israel. Vautours and Mystères were replaced by Skyhawks and Phantoms; Mirages by F-16s; Shermans and M3 half-tracks by M60 Pattons and M113 APCs – turning Israel into a regional superpower armed with nuclear weapons and the means to deliver them. Nasser's abiding legacy has been to fuse the United States of America and Israel in the minds of many Arabs into a single hateful entity with which dialogue is impossible and its destruction the only outcome. Furthermore, the Arab street has forsaken Nasser's pan-Arabism and shifted their allegiances to the certainties of the Mosque.

To the Egyptians, the Third Arab-Israeli War did not end on 9 June 1967. There was no Six Day War. It was simply *al-Naxa* – the setback. Resistance never faltered. On 1 July 1967, the Egyptian Army and Air Force mounted an incursion into the Sinai resulting in a victory at the village of Ras al Ush. On 21 October 1967, Egyptian missile boats sank the Israeli Navy destroyer, INS *Eilat*. This was 'The Period of Defiance and Persistence'. On 15 June 1968,

An Israeli soldier armed with a captured Kalashnikov assault rifle covers the dead bodies of Egyptian soldiers lost in the pitiless desert. Most have discarded their uniforms in a desperate attempt to escape the fighting and flee to their homes in Egypt.

the War of Attrition began in earnest. On 3 March 1969, President Nasser officially rescinded the ceasefire of 9 June 1967. On 7 August 1970, a ceasefire was agreed to end the War of Attrition – in reality the Fourth Arab-Israeli War – with both sides claiming victory (see Fortress 79: *Israeli Fortifications of the October War 1973* by Simon Dunstan, Osprey Publishing Ltd: Oxford, 2008). On 6 October 1973, both Egypt and Syria launched a combined offensive to restore their territories lost in the Six Day War. To this day, the Egyptians believe they were triumphant in the October War of 1973 (see *The Yom Kippur War: The Arab-Israeli War of 1973* by Simon Dunstan, Osprey Publishing Ltd: Oxford, 2007). In the Middle East, perception is everything.

THE BATTLEFIELD TODAY

It is extremely difficult to identify the battlefield at the Rafah Junction in which Brig. Gen. Tal's 84th Armored Division fought. First of all Rafah itself has changed from a small village of a couple of thousand inhabitants in 1967; it has become a giant complex numbering over 120,000 people. There are a number of densely packed refugee camps and housing projects, which have been built on some of the scenes of the Rafah battle. After the war, Israel established the Brazil and Canada housing projects to accommodate displaced Palestinians; Brazil Camp is to the immediate south of Rafah, where Col. Raful Eitan's paratroops entered Sinai and fought the flanks of the Egyptian 7th Infantry Division and the formidable IS-3 Stalin tanks. The abandoned Dahaniya airport can be seen just to the north. The ruins of the former Israeli settlements, evacuated in 2005, are visible between Rafah North and Khan Yunis, a large town complex where Kahalani's Pattons fought their bloody battle through the eastern outskirts towards the Gaza–Rafah road.

The ultimate prize for the IDF Southern Command was the Suez Canal despite the specific orders by Minister of Defense, Moshe Dayan, for Israeli forces to keep at least 16km (ten miles) from its banks to allow the Egyptians to maintain the territorial integrity of the international waterway. In the event, the Suez Canal was to remain closed until the spring of 1975.

The Egyptian-controlled border checkpoint is just west of the Israeli-constructed barrier called 'Philadelphi Corridor', the remnants of which can still be seen. The entire area along the border, in which the notorious Rafah subterranean 'tunnel city' has served as Hamas's main supply lifeline, is now a moonlike landscape, bombarded by countless air attacks during Operation *Cast Lead* of January 2009. Passing the checkpoint into Egyptian Sinai, the other part of Rafah City in Egypt can be seen. Here the smuggling commerce is booming and the town has grown accordingly.

On Road 30 leading towards El Arish, which has also become a major town complex, one passes the Jeradi defile over which heavy fighting surged as Gonen's 7th Armored Brigade raced towards El Arish, which was then a minor township but a major military location. On the road leading east towards Abu Ageila a major airport has been built and, not far from there, the Multi-National Forces Camp is located in El Gorah. Further west is the Bir Lahfan defile, where some of the fiercest tank vs. tank battles were fought. The scenery here has not changed and the battlefield can still be seen and followed clearly. Abu Ageila junction has not changed either, but is still an important doorway into central Sinai, although the road network has been modernized. The same applies to Brig. Gen. Sharon's Um Katef battle where the nature of the terrain is unchanged.

FURTHER READING

Aburish, Said K., *Nasser: The Last Arab* St Martin's Press: New York, 2004

Aloni, Shlomo, *Arab-Israeli Air Wars 1947–82* Osprey Publishing: Oxford, 2000

Aloni, Shlomo, *101 – Israeli Air Force First Fighter Squadron* IsreaDecal
    Publications: Israel, 2007

Black, Ian, and Benny Morris, *Israel's Secret Wars: A History of Israel's Intelligence
    Services* Grove Press: New York, 1991

Bowen, Jeremy, *Six Days: How the 1967 War Shaped the Middle East* Simon
    & Schuster: London ,2004

Bregman, Ahron, *Israel's Wars: A History since 1947* Routledge: London, 2000

Duncan, Andrew, and Michel Opatowski, *War in the Holy Land from Meggido
    to the West Bank* Sutton Publishing: Stroud, 1998

Dupuy, Trevor, *Elusive Victory: The Arab-Israeli Wars 1947–1974* Macdonald
    & Jane's: London, 1978

Eshcl, David, *The Edge of the Sword: Born in Battle* Eshcl-Dramit: Isracl, 1978

——, *Israel's Air Force: Born in Battle* Eshel-Dramit: Israel, 1978

——, *The Six Day War: Born in Battle* Eshel-Dramit: Israel, 1979

——, *Airborne & Commando Raids: Born in Battle* Eshel-Dramit: Israel, 1979

——, *Chariots of the Desert: The Story of the Israeli Armoured Corps* Brassey's:
    London, 1989

Ginor, Isabella, and Gideon Remez, *Foxbats over Dimona: The Soviets' Nuclear
    Gamble in the Six Day War* Yale University Press: New Haven, CT, 2007

Herzog, Chaim, and Shlomo Gazit, *The Arab-Israeli Wars: War and Peace in the
    Middle East* Greenhill Books: London, 2005

IDF Historical Branch, *Commanders of the Six Day War and their Battle Reports*
    Ramdor Publishing: Israel, 1967

Katz, Samuel M., *Israeli Elite Units since 1948* Osprey Publishing: Oxford, 1988

Luttwark, Edward, and Dan Horowitz, *The Israel Army* Allen Lane: London, 1975

Morris, Benny, *Righteous Victims: A History of the Zionist-Arab Conflict
    1881–1999* John Murray: London, 1999

O'Balance, Edgar, *The Third Arab-Israeli War* Faber and Faber: London, 1972

Oren, Michael B., *Six Days of War: June 1967 and the Making of the Modern
    Middle East* Oxford University Press: Oxford, 2002

Rothenberg, Gunther E., *The Anatomy of the Israeli Army* Batsford: London, 1979

Rubinstein, Murray and Richard Goldman, *The Israeli Air Force Story* Arms
    & Armour Press: London, 1978

Segev, Tom, *1967: Israel, the War and the Year that Transformed the Middle East*
    Little, Brown: London, 2007

Teveth, Shabtai, *The Tanks of Tammuz* Weidenfeld & Nicholson: London, 1969

Van Creveld, Martin, *The Sword and the Olive: A Critical History of the IDF*
    Perseus Book Group: New York, 1998

INDEX

References to illustrations are shown in **bold**.